"In this rohn ence, Tukufu
Zuberi uses interviews, newsreels, and archival sources to understand the
human experience in Africa and how Africans turned those experiences
into struggles that changed their lives. This is a critically important study of
Africa in the modern world." **—Tiffany Ruby Patterson, Vanderbilt
University**

"My dear friend, former Kenyan Prime Minister Raila Odinga, often
quotes a familiar African proverb: 'Until the lion speaks, the story of the
hunt will always glorify the hunter.' In *African Independence*, not only does
one of Africa's lions speak, but he roars. Zuberi demands our attention by
forcing us to see formerly obscured realities, and, in doing so, positions us to
better understand Africa's future. This book is eminently helpful in putting
Africa's past, present, and future in proper perspective." **—Ambassador
Charles R. Stith, former U.S. Ambassador to Tanzania; founder
and director, African Presidential Center at Boston University**

"*African Independence* and its accompanying documentary film are indispens-
able for anyone who desires to be a truly well-educated twenty-first-century citizen. This meticulously researched book reveals the contradictions
that continue to obstruct aspirations for African liberation. Indeed, the
evidence presented shows that Africa is 'once again locked in a death grip'
of postcolonial and postindependence manipulations. This book illuminates
not only how we are all implicated but that our own humanity depends on
how Africa shapes the world in this century." **—Joyce King, Benjamin
E. Mays Endowed Professor, Georgia State University**

"This book provides a valuable record of the aspirations, conflicts, and
confluences among a diverse array of actors, providing an opportunity
to consider the vast changes of both Africa and the world from the latter
half of the twentieth century to the twenty-first." **—Michael Hanchard,
Johns Hopkins University**

"Professor Zuberi has written an easy-to-read, absorbing, and welcomed
history of the African continent. He recounts how, over a long period of
time, the wealth of this continent has been, in a sense, stolen for European
usage rather than for the benefit of the local inhabitants. In a straightforward

tone he further underscores the abuse of the peoples both socially and economically and questions whether equal value was gained by Africa for their contribution to the other parts of the world." *—ImagineMag!: A South African Arts & Culture Magazine*

"As a historian, Zuberi's strength is not so much in chronicling and explaining history as it is in immersing himself in the lives of those who lived it. To write *African Independence*, the author spent years researching and traveling in Africa, interviewing everyone from political leaders to taxi drivers." *—The Wesleyan Argus*

"The main strength of this book lies in the author's ability to conduct oral interviews with leading African political figures, mostly from his *African Independence* documentary series. . . . I would recommend this book to the general reader interested in the history of postcolonial Africa, especially those interested in international relations and the challenges faced by the African postcolonial state." *—African Studies Quarterly*

AFRICAN INDEPENDENCE

How Africa Shapes the World

TUKUFU ZUBERI

ROWMAN & LITTLEFIELD
Lanham • Boulder • New York • London

Published by Rowman & Littlefield
A wholly owned subsidary of The Rowman & Littlefield Publishing Group, Inc.
4501 Forbes Boulevard, Suite 200, Lanham, Maryland 20706
www.rowman.com

Unit A, Whitacre Mews, 26-34 Stannary Street, London SE11 4AB,
United Kingdom

British Library Cataloguing in Publication Information Available

The Library of Congress cataloged the hardcover edition as follows:
Zuberi, Tukufu, author.
  African independence : how Africa shapes the world / Tukufu Zuberi.
    pages cm
  Includes bibliographical references and index.
    1. Africa—History—20th century. 2. Africa—History—21st century.
  3. Africa—Politics and government—1960- 4. Africa—Foreign relations—1960–
  5. Africa—Colonial influence. I. Title.
  DT31.Z83 2015
  960.3'2—dc23

                                                                    2015008575

ISBN 978-1-4422-1641-9 (cloth : alk. paper)
ISBN 978-1-4422-1642-6 (pbk. : alk. paper)
ISBN 978-1-4422-1643-3 (electronic)

∞™ The paper used in this publication meets the minimum requirements of
American National Standard for Information Sciences—Permanence of Paper
for Printed Library Materials, ANSI/NISO Z39.48-1992.

Printed in the United States of America

This book is dedicated to
Naima Margaret Zuberi
On her first birthday in
The hope that her bright
Eyes may one day see
The world
I dream.

CONTENTS

MAPS

ACKNOWLEDGMENTS

A book, like a film, is best when created in collaboration with others. This book benefited from several conversations and conferences with other scholars, activists, revolutionaries, freedom fighters, and artists, who helped me develop my thoughts.

Dr. Tamara K. Nopper read each chapter and provided me with important bibliographical, editorial, and substantive suggestions. Drs. Amson Sibanda, Alden Young, Clemmie L. Harris, and Tiffany R. Patterson read every page and gave me invaluable comments. Drs. Vanicléia Silva Santos and Rogaia Mustafa Abusharaf gave me important comments on selected parts of the manuscript, which greatly improved the text. Professor Michael Hanchard took valuable time from his research leave to read each chapter of the final version of the manuscript. His comments were crucial in my avoiding big gaps and hopefully helped in my final organization of the book.

I organized a conference on the social, political, and economic conditions in Africa from World War II through the periods of independence and the Cold War, which was held at the University of Pennsylvania and sponsored by the Center for Africana Studies and *The Annals of the American Academy of Political and Social Science*. This conference served as the basis for a special volume of *The Annals*, entitled "Perspectives on Africa and the World," and both the volume contributors and the presenters at the conference gave me important direction for the completion of the film and this book.

Films, unlike books, require a team. I was fortunate to work with several people over the past years on this project. The long credits following the film attest to the fact that I did not make the film on my own.

In part my ability to make the film and do the interviews for this book resulted from my work and collaborations on the African continent. These working relationships have been both academic and political. Examples of my academic and political collaborations are reflected in my work with Dr. Osman Sankoh, executive director of INDEPTH Network, and Professor Ayaga A. Bawah, also of INDEPTH Network; Pali Lehohla, statistician general of South Africa; and Dr. Collins Opiyo, director of population and social statistics of Kenya. Likewise, my participation in the African Presidential Roundtables organized by Ambassador Charles Stith enhanced my contact with African leaders. All these individuals and institutions helped me in critical and important ways in the production of this project. Finally, I must thank all of my colleagues at the University of Pennsylvania, especially those in the Department of Sociology and the Center for Africana Studies who have been so vital in my research. President Amy Gutmann has continued to support this project as it developed from an idea into the film and this book. Thanks also to Astrid Liliana Angulo Cortes for her inspiration.

Jabari Zuberi and Accra E. Zuberi were essential in the production of the book and the film. Jabari has been my travel companion, creative director, editor, and much more in the production of the film and the photos for the book. The photos were all shot by Jabari or myself, and edited by Jabari.

Accra provided the graphics that appear as the book cover, in the book, and in the film. She is also responsible for each of the maps. The

Speaking with African leaders at the African Presidential Roundtable in Dar es Salaam, Tanzania, 2010. Screenshot from *African Independence*.

With the ACAP and INDEPTH teams in Accra, Ghana, left to right, are Mr. Pali Lehohla, Dr. Alioune Diagne, Mr. Timothy Cheney, Ms. Samuelina Arthur, Dr. Tukufu Zuberi, Dr. Ayaga Bawah, Dr. Cheikh Mbacke, Dr. Martin Bangha, Dr. Philomena Nyarko, Mr. Somnath Sambhudas, Ms. Jeannette Quarcoopome, and Dr. Osman Sankoh, 2011. Jabari Zuberi/TZ Production Company.

US ambassador to Tanzania Charles Stith (1998–2001) speaks at the African Presidential Roundtable in Dar es Salaam, Tanzania, 2010. Jabari Zuberi/TZ Production Company.

xiv *Acknowledgments*

political context of each map resulted from our conversations and studies of historical maps. For some reason we have been engaged in a conversation about maps that has continued for as long as I can remember. It is truly a pleasure to be related to such creative people as Jabari and Accra.

The above individuals and institutions gave me many ideas and corrections that I was able to make thanks to their expert assistance. For the mistakes that remain, I take sole responsibility.

INTRODUCTION

I believe the inclusion of Africa in human history to be scientifically sound and necessary for logical social conclusions. In order to understand the world, we must understand Africa. The major events of the past require a more robust understanding of the events that have shaped the outcomes of history. Consider this: we cannot understand World War II, the fights against colonial domination, the Cold War, or the war against terrorism without a better understanding of Africa. I remind the reader that Africa has played a major role in human history and suggest that it is impossible to understand the present condition of humanity, or our future, without a consideration of Africa. Likewise, I firmly believe that African history is meaningless outside of the context of world history. By looking at the independence movement, we learn how events in Africa shape the world.

Africa is not only the cradle of all mankind but, unsurprisingly, also home to some of the world's most ancient civilizations. Over a billion people live in Africa, speaking some two thousand languages and dialects and living in some fifty-three different countries. Africa is so vast that you could put the landmasses of China, India, Argentina, New Zealand, and the continental United States within it and *still* not fill the entire continent. Africa stretches about five thousand miles from Cape Blanc in Tunisia to Cape Agulhas in South Africa and is divided into Southern, East, Central, West, and North Africa. The Sahara is the largest desert in the world, yet the vast stretch of African savannah land that spreads across twenty-five countries has the potential to turn several of its nations into major global economic players. While Africa is geographically one continent, politically, culturally, economically, and socially, it is more diverse than Europe, Asia, or the Americas. African mineral deposits are some of the largest and richest in the world, and the potential in Africa for the discovery and development

1

of mineral resources is immense. Africa supplies over half the world's diamonds, as well as large quantities of gold, uranium, platinum, and copper.

As we start, let me repeat that the real subject of this book is not African independence *tout court*, but rather African independence as part of a project to redefine what it means to be human in a world in which too much of the power and wealth remains in the hands of a very few people. Following World War II, the rise of US hegemony and the Cold War between the United States and the Soviet Union; the success of the independence movements in the Philippines, the Indian Subcontinent, and Indonesia; the Viet Minh defeat of the French; and the Communist Party's victory in China all transformed the geopolitics of the world. African Independence flourished in this new political environment. This project is one way that a professor, intellectual, and critic who is concerned about human rights, social justice, and equity looks at African independence in a time when Africa and the world are rife with war, with all kinds of terrorism, and with belligerent disregard for human dignity.

I begin these reflections by saying immediately that, for many compelling reasons, I shall be focusing on the experiences of African independence in the African republics of Tanzania, Kenya, South Africa, Ghana, and Zambia, although I do think that a good deal of my argument applies elsewhere too. The documentary that I produced to accompany the book, also titled *African Independence*, will provide an additional visual dimension of the story. If you have seen the film, you will find that the book places the narrative of the video into a broader context. The four chapters mirror the major ideas of the film.

WHY I WROTE THIS BOOK AND MADE A FILM

As a boy, I knew little of Africa. I grew up in Oakland, California, in the 1960s and 1970s and spent my childhood in the housing projects down the street from a Black Panther Party office. I saw the Panthers march and clash with the police and ate in the local breakfast programs that the Panthers sponsored. This experience gave me an interest in the social and political events of the world. The books that I read in high school had no information about Africa, and little attention was paid to world events in my classes. These high school books increased my ignorance about Africa and most of the world. Even what I knew about the United States was distorted. My high school experience was transformed by one of my teachers. In my senior year, my English teacher, Mrs. Clara Daniels, had us read a book on

Frederick Douglass, Booker T. Washington, and W. E. B Du Bois. This book inspired me to think in a broader fashion about the world than before.

A series of events changed my life: I entered college and learned more about civil rights and Black Power movements in the United States. In fact, I begin to connect the dots between the movements in the United States and movements in other parts of the world, like the anti-apartheid movement, the struggle in Zimbabwe (at the time Rhodesia), the revolution against the military juntas in El Salvador, the fight against the Somoza dictatorship by the Sandinista National Liberation Front, and the rise of the Black Power movements in Latin America, to name a few. Knowledge of the last remaining fights for independence led me to become actively involved in the divestment movement focused on South Africa, and I began to visit Africa on a regular basis. It was at college that I picked up W. E. B. Du Bois's seminal book, *The Negro*. This Pan-African scholar had produced the first modern effort to write a continental history of Africa. *The Negro* and other works by Du Bois have had a profound impact on how I view academic work. Like Du Bois, I am a student of sociology. As a professor, I have dedicated my career to writing about and studying Africa and the African diaspora. Like Du Bois, I am also interested in public education (Du Bois called such work propaganda). I have lived in the United States of America for my entire life, and for the past several decades as an active professor of sociology, demography, and Africana studies, an intellectual, critic, and proponent of human rights and social justice. This is the world I know best, and it has shaped my interactions with the world at large and with Africa in particular.

Second, as an African American citizen of the world's only remaining superpower, my intellectual interaction with the United States offers a special challenge and demands a more enlightened view of the world, unlike the difficulties confronted by other writers in other countries and from different backgrounds. I live in a society marked by colonialism, capitalism, racism, sexism, and large numbers of immigrants and veterans of numerous wars. The United States has never been a homogenous nation, and that, too, is part of the mix of factors that a serious person is required to take into account. Race, class, and gender continue to pose serious obstacles to equality, justice, and freedom in the US model of democracy and capitalism.

Third, I grew up as a marginalized racial subject in a major Western culture, and as someone who is especially attuned to perspectives and traditions other than those thought to be uniquely American or "Western." I operate effectively in the mainstream of the United States and the world, and in the waters of marginalization into which I am often thrown. I am simultaneously an American and part of the African diaspora. I am at the same time part of the superpower called the United States of America, yet I have been subject to forms of domination that have persisted in the United States since the days of enslavement. This has, I hope, made me a good listener as well as a good reader. For example, interpretations of African independence that derive from outside the Western purview interest me a great deal, and I shall be exploring them throughout the chapters. The reassertion of Africa and other non-European regions on the political scene was a significant accomplishment of the international movement for independence from classical colonialism.

Lastly, the world has changed considerably since the events of September 11, 2001, with dire consequences for most of humanity, and Africa is no exception. These changes have marked all of us in profound ways, and they continue to have an impact on our world today. The United States, the only remaining "superpower," has continued to frame its relationship to Africa in humanitarian rhetoric; therefore it is not surprising that the twenty-first century has borne witness to European and North American loss of political influence and economic advantages to the BRICS in Asia, Africa, and South America. I take these changes into consideration in chapter 4 where I discuss the prospects of extending African independence.

I have been a professor of sociology and Africana studies at the University of Pennsylvania since 1988. The University of Pennsylvania has offered me a privileged place to travel and view Africa and the world in the century that has just come to a close and the beginning of a new one. I recall organizing a conference on the study of Africa and the African diaspora with some colleagues, and I recall no less vividly being challenged by some scholars for daring to organize such a gathering in the United States.

For more than a decade, I have been a constant feature on television in the United States as a host on the long-running PBS series *History Detectives*, and later as a host and co-producer of PBS's *History Detectives: Special Investigations*, and more recently in other parts of the world as I have become an independent documentarian in Africa, Latin America, and elsewhere. I have screened and lectured about my film *African Independence* in numerous nations, and with the distribution of the film and this book, I am beginning to recognize the potential of a new model of academic production. These efforts at extending my educational practice to public education have naturally grown out of my curatorial experiences at major museums. These curatorial efforts include *Tides of Freedom: African Presence on the Delaware River*, which features newly uncovered artifacts from the Independent Seaport Museum's collection organized around four key moments in Philadelphia's history representing the themes of enslavement, emancipation, Jim Crow, and civil rights, and *Black Bodies in Propaganda: The Art of the War Poster*, which presents thirty-three posters from my personal collection, mostly targeting Africans and African American civilians in times of war. In addition to the posters, the *Black Bodies in Propaganda* exhibition featured interactive touch screens, archival military recruitment films from Europe and the United States, and a related segment from PBS's *History Detectives*. These activities have extended my classroom to the world. This extension of my work provides me with the background for my inquiry into the relevance of African independence to the contemporary world, the subject to which these pages are dedicated. It also indicates how this issue is contested with all sorts of debates, polemics, and research projects concerning how events in Africa have shaped the world, and been shaped by the world, in the closing half of the past century, and the impact these have had on the beginning of this one.

As a professor and researcher, I have cultivated a respect for how the past impacts our current society. My experience in broadcast television and as an independent documentary film producer has deepened my appreciation for the importance of archival materials in how we remember the past. Records of current events and the objects of the day become the documents of the past and open a window to interpreting history. This book is about memory in Africa—not just any kind of reflection on the memory of Africans, but a reflection on what Michael Hanchard describes as recollections of "circumstances, people, and institutions that brought them trauma, humiliation, disgrace, violence, and hardship."[1] These are recollections of experiences that changed their lives for the better, that made them move beyond the "pass laws" of South Africa and the racially segregated housing policies of Rhodesia (currently Zimbabwe) and South-West Africa (currently Namibia). I will also consider the circumstances, people, and institutions that brought solutions to African problems and produced the African independence movement.

MY POINT OF VIEW

Throughout I shall be mindful of what sociologist C. Wright Mills referred to as the problems of biography, history, and how they interact within society.[2] These three coordinate points of biography, history, and society are my platform, while my film and this book are my method of presentation.

In this consideration of African independence, I am interested in a better understanding of individual biography that is sociologically grounded and historically relevant. I see the African independence movement as a net-work of individuals, groups, and organizations engaged in a political strug-gle to enhance freedom, justice, and equality on the African continent.[3]

Europe and Asia have long had contact with what we know today as Africa. The Greeks knew of some, though not all, Africans, such as the An-cient Egyptians, and west of Egypt were the "Libyes" (Libyans) of the north and the "Aithiops" (Ethiopians) of the south. The Romans later referred to what they knew of the continent as "Afri." Thus, Africa, "the land of the Afri," originally referred to the Roman province established after the Roman conquest of Carthage in 146 BC. Following the fall of Rome and the rise of the Arabic language and Islam in the seventh century AD, the northern parts of the continent became known as "Ifriqiya" to the world. The Arabs had extensive knowledge and interaction with other parts of Africa below the Saharan Desert. The Arab slave trade in African people included populations from West, East, Central, and Southern Africa. In the fifteenth century (the "Age of Discovery"), with the Portuguese voyages, the term "Africa" was applied to what we now know as the entire conti-nent. The Portuguese opened the gates of Africa to European merchants and politicians in a new way, which entailed a new way of thinking about Africa.[4] This new way of thinking initiated a process that transformed both Africa and the world.

The context in which this change of thought and action occurred was slavery. The point to understand here is that the modern idea of Africa emerged, in many ways, from dehumanizing crucibles. Meanwhile, in Eu-rope and the United States, ideas about freedom and liberty were finding a new voice in the French and American Revolutions. In the Declaration of Independence, written by Thomas Jefferson in 1776, he claimed, "We hold these truths to be self-evident, that all men are created equal, that they are endowed by their creator with certain unalienable rights, that among these are life, liberty and the pursuit of happiness."

The French Declaration of the Rights of Man and of the Citizen in 1789, the preamble to the new French constitution, declared "the natural inalienable and sacred rights of man" to "liberty, property, security and resistance to oppression." In the West, "the rights of man" first appear in Rousseau's writings in the social contract; he apparently only used the term once, and he never really defined what it meant. Like its predecessor, "natural rights," "the rights of man" required no definition and maintained the tendency to be asserted as what Lynn Hunt calls a claim of "self-evident truths" in her book *Inventing Human Rights: A History.*

Although ideas of democracy were taking root in several European and American nations, Germany, France, and Britain required justifications for the mistreatment of Africa and Africans. And this is what led the greatest of European philosophers, the German Georg Hegel, to write in the 1830s that "what we properly understand by Africa is the Unhistorical, Undeveloped Spirit, still involved in the conditions of mere nature, and which had to be presented here only as on the threshold of the World's History."[5] Hegel's ignorance of the African map was more political than factual. Europe and the world were long aware of the realities of African life, and the reality of African civilizations prior to European contact was not new. However, the dawn of the new age of imperialism seems to have been open for such interpretations.

The age of imperialism occurred during the late nineteenth and early twentieth centuries. During this era, Western European nations, especially France and Britain, pursued aggressive policies to extend their political and economic control around the world. In the 1890s, Joseph Chamberlain gave new life to "imperialism" in his capacity as the British colonial secretary who championed British expansionist policies. This new imperialism was also reflected in new European policies like those of Jules Ferry, the prime minister of France, during the same period. The British economist J. A. Hobson's *Imperialism*, written in 1902, and Vladimir Lenin's *Imperialism as the Highest Stage of Capitalism*, written in 1917, are key examples of critiques from the left. Yet the West maintained that imperialism was the only way to spread civilization in the world's underdeveloped areas. The words of colonial secretary Joseph Chamberlain illustrate this point most clearly: "One great cause for the prosperity for the United States of America, admitted by every one to be a fact, is that they are a great empire of over 70,000,000 of people; that the numbers of these people alone, without any assistance from the rest of the world, would insure a large amount of prosperity. Yes; but the British Empire is even greater than the United States of America. We have a population—it is true, not all a white population—but we have a white population of over 50,000,000 against the 70,000,000—who are not all white, by-the-bye—(laughter)—against the 70,000,000 of America. We have, in addition, 350,000,000 or more of people under our protectorate, under our civilization, sympathizing with our rule, grateful for the benefits we accord to them, and all of them, more or less prospective or actual customers of this country."[6] The political map of Africa was transformed by actions that accompanied these ideas.

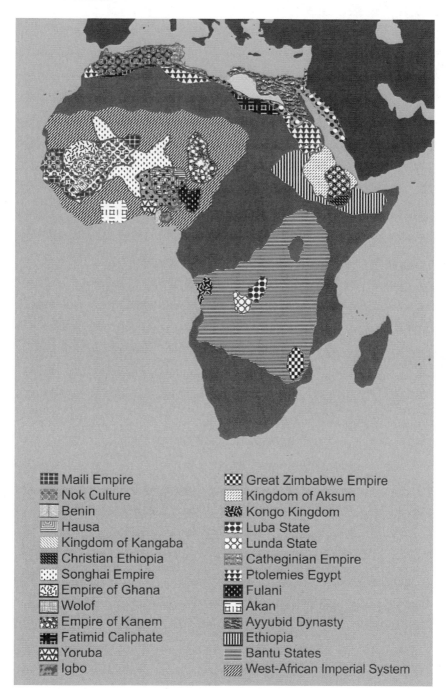

▦	Maili Empire	▦	Great Zimbabwe Empire
▨	Nok Culture	▨	Kingdom of Aksum
▧	Benin	▨	Kongo Kingdom
▣	Hausa	▦	Luba State
▧	Kingdom of Kangaba	▨	Lunda State
▦	Christian Ethiopia	▨	Catheginian Empire
▨	Songhai Empire	▦	Ptolemies Egypt
▨	Empire of Ghana	▦	Fulani
▦	Wolof	▤	Akan
▨	Empire of Kanem	▨	Ayyubid Dynasty
▦	Fatimid Caliphate	▥	Ethiopia
▨	Yoruba	▤	Bantu States
▨	Igbo	▨	West-African Imperial System

Pre-Colonial Africa, before 1600

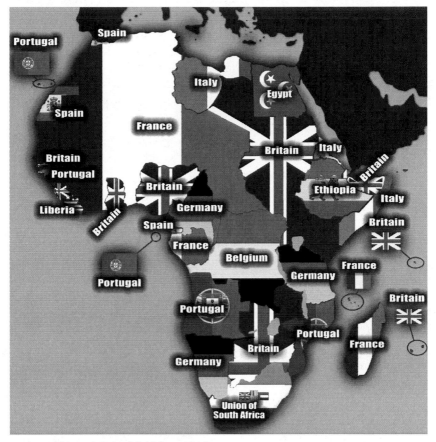

Pre–World War I Colonial Africa, 1914

How we document the past is a contested space. The official story depends on who has the authority to speak. Government recollections of the past are often at odds with those of people marginalized in society. Public recollections of past events are heavily influenced by the objects and images used to recall these past events, and visual images play a big part in this process.

In this book, I rely heavily on three types of recollections of the past: interviews, newsreels (including modern news and reports), and previous research. I include interviews conducted over a seven-year period on the African continent, and interviews and speeches from various video archives. Newsreel was a major form of short documentary of filmed news stories about issues of the day. It remained a major source of current affairs for millions of moviegoers until television assumed this role in the 1950s. The newsreel offers a brilliant example of the documentation of events that led up to World War II. They were also the foundation on which modern reporting and what passes as "news" developed. These interviews and newsreels serve as an essential part of my narrative.

HOW I TELL THE STORY

Understanding the reality of Africa in the twenty-first century requires viewing the continent within a broader context of recent world history. Through the lens of four watershed events—World War II, the end of colonialism, the Cold War, and the new global interconnections—*African Independence* shows how Africa is shaped as much by what happens in America, Europe, Russia, and China as it is by events within its own geographic borders. It also reveals how much the rest of the world is shaped by events in Africa. The four watershed events that changed the course of African and world history provide the focus for this project as well as the organizing principal for the book. The entire project has been conceived in four segments that coincide with the watershed events. This book is not simply about what Africa has been, nor is it simply a tract on what Africa is; instead, I consider what Africa can be in light of Africa's place in the world.

I have neither the desire nor the capacity to recapitulate all the arguments nor to undertake a catalog of the interpretations of African independence, except to note their encroaching presence on what I have to say and to indicate that I shall be making highly selective use of what others have said. Therefore, what follows in my first chapter is an extended meditation on the antecedents of African independence rather than a list of desirable attributes of what independence means, giving a whole series of claims and counterclaims made on behalf of the people of Africa by those who propose it as something about which they can speak. This chapter examines how Africa's relationship with the world was transformed through the participation of African soldiers in the Allied victory of World War II. In the aftermath of the war, Africans who had been fighting in Africa, Europe, and Asia for their colonial masters returned home with new calls for independence and democracy. African aspirations and the new world powers would prove to be the deathblow for classical European colonialism in Africa. This represents the first level of the contradictions between capitalism in the form of European colonialism and democracy on the African continent.

My second chapter investigates the roots of the African independence movement. In this chapter I consider the impact of the movement on the African imagination and on reality. Rather than give the reader a chronology of the movement, I attempt to link the rise of the movement for independence to the end of classical European colonialism. Even the most pessimistic reader must come to terms with the end of colonialism as a way of understanding African agency in the post–World War II period. This chapter looks at different manifestations of the African struggle to gain independence across the continent in the immediate post-war period. New leaders with democratic dreams for their new nations gave Africa and the world hope. At such a moment in history, everything seemed possible.

The third chapter reveals how the dream of independence turned sour once superpower attention turned to Africa during the Cold War. The chapter shows how and why Africa's potential was stifled when the continent became a proxy battleground between East and West. African leaders were raised up or thrown down based on their value to America or the Soviet Union.

The final chapter explores how the fall of the Berlin Wall and the end of the Cold War unleashed new energies across Africa with both great and terrible results. In this new era, African independence found a new symbol in Nelson Mandela, and the people's voices were heard all over the continent as never before. Yet the picture was complicated by genocide, regional wars, growing ethnic and religious fundamentalism, and the continued fight against poverty and disease.

In order to tell this story, I interviewed many contemporary leaders, revolutionaries, and leading personalities from the period. In fact, *African Independence* is based on years of research and travel in Africa as a political activist and scholar. With unprecedented access to "history makers," *African Independence* takes the form of a journey. Traveling by plane, bus, and cab to the locations where history was made, I guide the reader through a chronological narrative from World War II to the present. Across four chapters, I reveal the modern history, culture, and politics of Africa in a deeply personal way. With a strong emphasis on the African voice, I show how Africa's recent past provides a context to understand the continent as a whole, explaining its present realities and suggesting how it will impact the world's future.

The present plight of Africa is a direct outgrowth of the past, and certain ignorance of the historical record current in our day leads to a tragic failure in assessing causes. More importantly, the habit of ignoring the acts and social movements of the people of Africa not only is the cause of our present problem but will continue to cause trouble until we come to terms with Africa's place in the world. I do not want to exaggerate the role of African history in world development, but I will insist that Africa's role has been critical.

1

FROM COLONIALISM
TO PAN-AFRICANISM

The Impact of World War II

In researching this book and its documentary companion, I strove to dig deeper than the traditional commentaries that paint Africa as a poor continent that needs assistance and instead to find sources that illustrate both the strengths and the challenges that Africans face today, as well as their historic roots. I drew on more than three decades of work in Africa to connect with unusual sources and real people, from freedom fighters to taxi drivers. With the help of my friends and colleagues, I sought to discover what African leaders and politicians think about Africa's relationship with the rest of the world and how best to address the critical challenges facing the continent. When I began my research, the working title of my book and film were "Africa and the World"; however, it became clear over time that the title had to change. Perhaps the most interesting, if not remarkable, result of my journey has been the discovery that no matter whom I spoke to, the issue of African independence became a center of focus. African independence always seemed to be in deep and terminal trouble. The "crisis" in Africa could somehow always be traced to issues not adequately handled before and after Africa gained independence. African independence was part of an international movement that grew rapidly following the end of World War II. Understanding the roots of the movement in Africa may help us understand the implications that this movement has continued to have in the African imagination of freedom, justice, and equality.

World War II was a global turning point and a deathblow to classical European colonialism in Africa as documented by the decisive role played by African soldiers in the Allied victory. Just as African American soldiers fighting overseas returned from saving democracy in Europe to fight for civil rights at home, so too did African soldiers who fought on behalf of their colonial masters come back demanding control over their own destiny. I conclude this chapter by turning my attention to an event that happened at the same historical moment, when leaders of Africans and African descendants met in Manchester, England, in 1945 to consider the next steps at the Pan-African Congress. Like World War II, this congress was a catalyst for the independence movement spreading like fire across the African continent.

In 1935, newsreels indicated that Adolf Hitler was not yet ready to invade Africa. However, his fellow fascist in Italy, Benito Mussolini, was itching to punish Ethiopia for rejecting his invitation to join the new Italian Empire. So, Mussolini promised his people a new imperial greatness that was to be established by conquering Ethiopia.[1]

Arbitrations by the League of Nations failed. Neither of the world's two main superpowers of the time, the French Republic or Great Britain, was prepared to do more than offer political support. The League of Nations condemned the invasion and imposed sanctions on Italy; however, the sanctions were weak and ineffective without superpower support. The League of Nations, an international organization of governments founded after World War I as a result of the 1919 Treaty of Versailles, was charged with upholding the rights of the colonized and disempowered. It was also supposed to prevent war by settling disputes between countries through negotiations. Like the Mukden Incident in 1931, in which the Japanese annexed three Chinese provinces (also considered an important early provocation of the Second Sino-Japanese War), the so-called Second Italo-Abyssinian War foreshadowed the coming of the Second World War and the ineffectiveness of the League of Nations. The Second Italo-Abyssinian War and the fascist Italian colonial creation of the African Orientale Italiana (AOI) were clear examples of Italy defying the League.[2]

Both Ethiopia and Italy were member nations, yet the League was unable to stop the latter's aggression or to protect Ethiopia as outlined in the League's Article X. Article X of the League of Nations was a covenant providing for assistance to be given to member states in cases of external aggression. This is why Emperor Haile Selassie declared in his 1936 speech to the League of Nations,

> I, Haile Selassie I, Emperor of Ethiopia, am here today to claim that justice which is due to my people, and the assistance promised to it eight months ago, when fifty nations asserted that aggression had been committed in violation of international treaties.[3]

If the requested intervention were to happen, it would have been due to the efforts of the two main world powers. Britain and France could have closed the Suez Canal to Italian ships transporting troops, but France was treaty bound to Italy not to oppose the invasion, and Britain's foreign secretary feared that alienating Italy's Mussolini would drive him into the arms of Hitler. The newsreels of the time brilliantly document the Ethiopian people alone in their military confrontation with the more than four hundred thousand soldiers and superior weaponry of the fascist army.

A border dispute with Ethiopia over the Ogaden, a region in the Italian colony of Somaliland on the border of Ethiopia, was declared, and the first armed conflict broke out in the Wal Wal region in November and December 1934. Mussolini had contrived the perfect "incident" in the city of Wal Wal, and in doing so he created a perfect pretext for war. In December 1934, the dispute turned violent, and 107 Ethiopians, 50 Italians, and the Somalis fighting for Italy were killed. As Emperor Selassie noted in his League of Nations speech,

> The Wal-Wal incident, in December, 1934, came as a thunderbolt to me. The Italian provocation was obvious and I did not hesitate to appeal to the League of Nations. I invoked the provisions of the treaty of 1928, the principles of the Covenant; I urged the procedure of conciliation and arbitration. Unhappily for Ethiopia this was the time when

Emperor Haile Selassie of Ethiopia addresses the League of Nations in Geneva, Switzerland, circa 1936. Screenshot from *African Independence*.

Benito Mussolini justifying the Italian invasion of Ethiopia, 1935. Screenshot from *African Independence.*

Ethiopian soldiers preparing to confront Italian troops, 1935. Screenshot from *African Independence.*

a certain Government considered that the European situation made it imperative at all costs to obtain the friendship of Italy. The price paid was the abandonment of Ethiopian independence to the greed of the Italian Government. This secret agreement, contrary to the obligations of the Covenant, has exerted a great influence over the course of events. Ethiopia and the whole world have suffered and are still suffering today its disastrous consequences.

Italy refused arbitration from the League of Nations and mobilized its formidable army, navy, and air force, with Ethiopia left to her own forces to fight the might of Europe's strongest air force.

FASCIST WAR ON ETHIOPIA

On October 3, 1935, Mussolini's fascist troops marched into Ethiopia, one of the two areas in Africa not under European colonialism, the other being Liberia. The Italian dictator desired a new empire comparable to Rome, one that would rule over the Mediterranean and North Africa. He desired what the fascists of Italy referred to as the African Orientale Italiana. Ethiopia had become a symbol of African nationhood and an exception to the rule of Africa's second-class status in the world. It escaped the "Scramble for Africa" by the European nations at the end of the nineteenth century, making it one of two African states not subject to the rule of a European power. In addition, and important to Mussolini, was the March 1, 1896, Italian invasion of Ethiopia. In this historic "Battle of Adwa," Ethiopia inflicted a humiliating defeat on the invading military. Mussolini had promised his people a place in the colonial sun, matching the empires of Britain and France, and he used the historical defeat of 1896 as a call to arms in 1935.

In 1935, Ethiopia was militarily weak. Emperor Haile Selassie called for a general mobilization of the Army of the Ethiopian Empire. Selassie's army was composed of the Imperial Bodyguard, a central army, and several provincial armies. The majority of its soldiers were largely armed with spears, shields, and guns from the Battle of Adwa some forty years earlier. The Ethiopian air force was composed of only twelve aircraft. Italy on the other hand was eager to show the world its military strength. The Italian colonization of Ethiopia would unify the Italian colonies in Eritrea and Italian Somaliland.

With these weaknesses and political considerations in mind, the fascists, under the command of the Italian marshals Rodolfo Graziani and

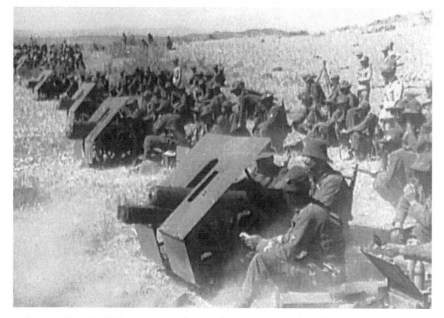

Italian soldiers in Ethiopia, 1935. Screenshot from *African Independence*.

Pietro Badoglio, attacked the independent African nation of Ethiopia. Mussolini's troops entered Ethiopia through Adwa in the north and Mogadishu in the south. They easily took Tigre. While his troops were in the heat of battle, Mussolini stood in Rome's Piazza Venezia and declared,

> I refuse to believe that the true people of France . . . and of Great Britain want to spill blood and push Europe on the road to catastrophe in order to defend an African country universally stamped as unworthy of taking its place with civilized people.

How correct he was about the European response. In December, France and Britain came together in Paris and agreed on the Hoare-Laval Plan, which amounted to abandoning the Ethiopian people.[4]

The walls vibrated; the ground shook. People poured into the streets. Looking up toward the sky, they observed the intense bombardments, which destroyed towns, villages, and livestock. The same bombs were captured on newsreels and seen all over the world. On April 9, 1936, a major Italian victory was won near Lake Ashangi. A month later on May 5, Addis Ababa fell, and Ethiopia's Emperor Haile Selassie took refuge in England.

Africa Orientale Italiana was born with the merger of Ethiopia and the Italian colonies of Somaliland and Eritrea.

The emperor of Ethiopia was born Tafari Makonnen on July 23, 1892, to Woizero Yshimebet Ali Abajifar, daughter of a famous Oromo leader, and Ras Makonnen Woldemikael Gudessa, a war hero from the Battle of Adwa. He claimed royal blood through his paternal grandmother, Princess Tenagnework Sahle Selassie, an aunt of Emperor Menelik II. Menelik II claimed direct uninterrupted male descent from Menelik I, who, according to Ethiopian tradition, was the offspring of King Solomon and the queen of Sheba. When he was crowned emperor in 1930, Tafari Makonnen took the name Haile Selassie, which means "Power of the Trinity." In a defining moment, His Imperial Majesty Haile Selassie I, King of Kings, Lord of Lords, Conquering Lion of the Tribe of Judah, and Elect of God, in his aforementioned 1936 speech to the League of Nations, condemned the Italian invasion of his country and the use of chemical weapons. The archival footage of this historic moment shows a proud Selassie marching to the podium and admonishing the Western powers in attendance with the words, "I must still fight on until my tardy allies appear, and if they never come, I say to you without bitterness, the West will perish."

According to British newspapers, the Ethiopians cabled the League of Nations that the first bombs struck a hospital bearing the Red Cross. Italy dropped an estimated 317 tons of chemicals on the defenseless Ethiopians. In its bombing and poison gassing, Italy violated the Geneva Protocol of 1925, among other international laws. While the unprovoked barbarities led to international moral outrage, Europe did not rise to the occasion. When the League of Nations accused Mussolini's military of targeting Red Cross medical tents, Mussolini responded that the Ethiopians were not fully human; therefore no human rights were violated and human rights laws were not applicable. Mussolini's comments underlay the rationale for colonialism in Africa. How else could Belgium, France, Britain, and Portugal justify their African colonies? The hypocrisy of colonialism was exploited by the fascist desires to redistribute the colonial territories of the world.

After seven months of war, Ethiopia was forcibly united with Eritrea and Somaliland to give Italy an East African empire. In Rome, Mussolini proclaimed the king of Italy, Victor Emmanuel III, as "emperor of Ethiopia." However, the Ethiopian Empire never capitulated or surrendered, and His Imperial Majesty Haile Selassie fled into exile. Some argue that the lack of capitulation by the emperor and the continued resistance during the Italian occupation challenge the idea that Ethiopia was colonized during this period. Major Western nations, including Britain, France, and Italy, refused to acknowledge or defend the human rights of the people of Ethiopia. The proof of which was the Italian use of chemical weapons and the refusal by Britain and France to honestly support the activation of the non-aggression clauses of the League of Nations. In the face of all this, Haile Selassie continued to assert his people's humanity.

The occupation of Ethiopia was followed by the legalization of racism in everyday life. As of April 19, 1937, it was illegal for whites to marry blacks. And the grand design for urban development included plans for segregating the colonized from the settlers. Finally, consistent with their fellow imperial powers, the fascist government took the best local land and redistributed it to Italian settlers. Mussolini announced, "Italy finally had its own empire. A Fascist empire, a peaceful empire, an empire of civilization and humanity." The Italian nation embraced the song "Faccetta nera," which included the lines

> Little black face, pretty Abyssinian girl, you wait and hope, and already Italy is approaching. When we are there in your company we shall give you a different set of laws and a different King.

Mussolini appointed Marshal Badoglio as viceroy of Italy. A large number of Italian troops maintained martial law and fought the resistance that continued to pose a threat in the southwest. Britain signed a secret agreement with Italy in an effort to avoid war with the fascists; however, Mussolini and Hitler signed the "Pact of Steel" three years later. The Pact of Steel was designed for an attack against British interests in the Mediterranean.[5]

The East African campaign was a total war against the Ethiopian people. The Italians were indiscriminate and fought civilians and soldiers, killing and wounding women as well as children. This was a war of occupation, of repression, of exploitation, and, in some ways, of extermination. The daily lives and the very existence of the Ethiopian people were disrupted. The people were deprived of food, freedom, and their national independence and were full of fear. Wars of colonial occupation were not unknown in Africa, of course, far from it. Dating back to the Berlin Conference of the late 1880s, colonial occupation became a part of the African social consciousness; military forces from France, Britain, Germany, and Italy terrorized African populations and preserved the colonial empires of Europe. However, unique to the Ethiopian invasion was that it served as Africa's introduction to what the world would come to recognize as World War II.

Africa's baptism into the conflict that would escalate into World War II began with Mussolini's invasion of Ethiopia. World War II continued into the East and North African campaigns and did not end until the war's later stages. Four years after the Italian attack on Ethiopia, the war escalated in Europe when Hitler's military invaded Poland in September 1939. As full-scale world war raged in Europe, Africa was transformed into combat zones, and military mobilization affected the lives of millions of men and women.

It was not until June 10, 1940, that Italy declared war on Great Britain and France, thereby aligning with Germany. The very next day the North African campaign began with the Italian offensive against British forces based in Egypt. Libya was already part of the African Orientale Italiana. Only the French colony in Algeria, along with their protectorate of Tunisia and a narrow part of the Mediterranean, broke the Axis supply line between Germany and Egypt.

Italy was poised to challenge the British and French as the main colonial powers on the African continent. Mussolini turned his military attention to Egypt. The Egyptian Nile and Suez Canal would be political and strategic victories, comparable to the advances made by Mussolini's Nazi partners in Europe. He sent a large number of troops into Libya, Egypt's neighbor, and another large force into the newly occupied Ethiopia. Italy was poised to confront the smaller British forces in the Western Desert Force.

In the south, the Italian armies in Ethiopia, Eritrea, and Somalia were under the Duke of Aosta, viceroy of Ethiopia and supreme commander. In Ethiopia, the Italian military included 91,000 Italian and 199,000 African troops. British troops were scattered thinly along the wide frontiers of Egypt, the Sudan, Kenya, and British Somaliland. The Butcher of Libya, Marshal Graziani, invaded Egypt on September 13, 1940, with an army of eighty thousand Italians and conscripted Libyans. They overwhelmed the British troops, forcing them to withdraw to Mersa Matruh. The fascists advanced up to Sidi Barrāni, which they occupied three days later. The Italian military was eighty miles west of the British forces in Mersa Matruh and three hundred miles from Cairo.

A few months earlier in July, the Italians took Moyale on the Kenya-Ethiopia border and began an advance toward Buna and Lake Rudolf. On August 4, the Italian army invaded British Somaliland and occupied the protectorate. In turn, the British continued to work with the African opposition in Ethiopia to foster the eventual return of Emperor Selassie.

In the autumn of 1940, when the Battle for Britain against German occupation was at its height, Italy attacked Egypt. While the Italian forces stalled in Sidi Barrāni, the central Italian unit in command of the military switched its focus from Egypt to the Italian invasion of Greece on October 28. This new situation led to the Italian forces' delaying their invasion of

Mersa Matruh in Egypt. They rescheduled the invasion to occur on December 15. However, on December 8, the British caught the Italians totally off guard by attacking their forces in Sidi Barrāni. The Italian pause in fighting had allowed the British forces time to plan a counterattack. The British surprise attack took four days to succeed. The smaller Western Desert Force took another six weeks to push the Italian army as far as El Agheila, less than one hundred miles outside of Tripoli.

A large Sudanese contingent fought with the British and Ethiopians in the liberation of Ethiopia in 1941. Ethiopian troops were organized under the command of Colonel Wingate with the name "Gideon Force." In the liberation of Ethiopia, the Gideon Force penetrated Gojam. In Tigre, General Platt, starting out from the Sudan, took Keren in Somaliland. General Cunningham set out from Kenya and captured Harar and then Addis Ababa. The various troops met up on the Amba Alaguir. The Duke of Aosta surrendered, and the path for Haile Selassie's return was set.

Emperor Selassie crossed the border into Ethiopia near a village called Um Iddla. After joining with the other resistance forces in the country, the Ethiopian troops raised the standard of the Lion of Judah, and next the emperor and the Army of Ethiopian Free Forces entered Addis Ababa. Ethiopia and her allies, as tardy as they may have been, were able to defeat the Italian efforts at colonization. In 1943, after a lengthy guerrilla war, the remnants of Italy's troops and their Ethiopian allies were expelled from Ethiopia, followed by the formal surrender of Italy.

The East African campaign was over. The fascist war in Africa began with Mussolini's invasion of Ethiopia in 1935 and ended five years later when Ethiopian freedom fighters brought an end to the East African campaign with the assistance of Allied forces.

The independence of Ethiopia was reestablished, but Somaliland remained a British colonial possession. Both Italian Somaliland and Eritrea were placed under British administration. After the end of what was now World War II, Italian Somaliland became the Trust Territory of Somalia under Italian administration. The idea of the Trust Territory would become problematic in Africa. This problem was worsened by Ethiopia's annexation of Eritrea in 1952, an act that would lead to years of war between the peoples of Eritrea and Ethiopia.

NORTH AFRICA CAMPAIGN

With victory in the East African campaign, the North African campaign took on a new urgency. In this campaign, the Afrika Korps under the leadership of Marshal Erwin Rommel had joined Italy in the fight. This German expeditionary force had begun arriving in Tripoli from Palermo, Sicily. On March 20, Rommel met with Hitler in Berlin and was ordered to launch an offensive against the British as soon as the German troops had all landed in Tripoli. Rommel arrived and led the fascist forces in several strategic victories, which placed the British on the defensive. However, this all changed when the German and Italian supply convoys were stopped by the British, who were then joined by their US allies in 1942, two years into the North African campaign against the Axis Powers. After years in opposition to European colonialism, even the traditional Sanusi leaders from Libya returned to fight on the side of the Allies during this important campaign.

The Sanusi had long been engaged in battle with the Italians over the control of what is now recognized as part of Libya. As early as 1922, Mussolini's new government pursued a strong policy of Italian settlement in north and northeast Africa. The Libyan protectorate was annexed as a colony by Italy, forming the Tripolitania Italiana, Cyrenaica Italiano, and Fezzan Italiano. During this time, the Sanusi resisted Italian colonization in what was known as Cyrenaica. By the time of the North African campaign, over 150,000 Italians had settled in Libya.

Around this same time, Germany had defeated the French. During the Nazi occupation of France from 1940 to 1944, the Vichy regime was in "power." The Vichy regime was an ally of Nazi Germany. General Philippe Pétain, a French World War I hero, was the leader of the regime, which took its name from the government's capital in Vichy, southeast of Paris, near Clermont-Ferrand. The Vichy regime was a puppet state that collaborated with the Nazis and was challenged by the Free French forces of Charles de Gaulle. De Gaulle had been Pétain's protégé.

The German forces were also on the offensive in North Africa when President Franklin Delano Roosevelt and Prime Minister Winston Churchill first met on Placentia Bay, off Newfoundland close to the port of Argentina, on the US battle cruiser *Augusta*. Roosevelt suggested a joint Anglo-American declaration of principles linking British war objectives with US political aspirations, even though the United States was still not a party to the war. Churchill handed Roosevelt a draft declaration during their second meeting on August 10, 1941, held on board the camouflaged British ship, the *Prince of Wales*. Roosevelt insisted that the document, which became known as the Atlantic Charter, proclaimed the right of all people to self-determination in the name of democracy and freedom. In the charter, Britain and the United States pledged to "respect the right of all peoples to choose the form of government under which they will live;

British prime minister Winston Churchill (right) greeting President Franklin Delano Roosevelt (left) on board the USS *Augusta*, 1941. Screenshot from *African Independence*.

and they wish to see sovereign rights and self-government restored to those who have been forcibly deprived of them."[6]

On November 8, 1942, the Allies landed in the Vichy French territories of Algeria and Morocco. The Allies, and their African allies, captured Casablanca on the Atlantic coast and Oran and Algiers on the Mediterranean coast. They quickly dispatched the French forces loyal to Vichy and the fascists. The Allies landed in French North Africa as Rommel and his Afrika Korps were in full retreat. The end of the North African campaign was near. By 1943, when the campaign came to an end, the battle in North Africa had cost both sides over 100,000 soldiers, and over 130,000 Germans left for prisoner-of-war camps.[7]

Meanwhile back in Europe, the peoples who fell under Nazi rule were either put to work for the Reich or selected for extermination and destruction. From the African point of view, this was a case of the chickens coming home to roost in Europe, as overseas in Asia and Africa, European states habitually indentured and enslaved Asian and African populations for their own industrial and governmental benefit. Belgium, Portugal, France,

Britain, and the other colonizers used torture, mutilation, and mass murder to coerce Africans into submission.

AFRICAN CONTRIBUTIONS TO THE WAR EFFORT

The African colonies provided essential manpower and material for the war effort. Several colonies were the theaters of major military operations: Ethiopia, Egypt, Libya, Tunisia, Algeria, Morocco, and Somalia. The continent also played a vital strategic role in World War II by providing staging bases for British, American, and other Allied soldiers and supplies en route to Asia.[8]

African soldiers in colonial French service were called "Tirailleurs Sénégalais." Despite the name, Tirailleurs Sénégalais included soldiers from throughout French West Africa. Like the African American troops of the United States, African troops were organized in segregated regiments as part of the French Colonial Army, or La Coloniale. French officers or, on occasion, an African junior officer commanded them. African junior officers constituted a small minority of the French army.

In addition to the large number of Tirailleurs Sénégalais, the French Colonial Army also included the smaller Malagasy Tirailleurs, the Algerian Tirailleurs, and the Moroccan Tirailleurs. The French Colonial Army also consisted of European men recruited from the settler population living throughout colonial French Africa. This Army of Africa, or Armee d'Afrique, should not be confused with the various Tirailleurs, as Africans were not allowed to join this exclusive white branch of the French Colonial Army.

The fascists were aware of the African threat. African participation in the war gave the European colonial powers access to millions of soldiers and support staff. In *Mein Kampf*, Hitler criticized the French for "polluting" their once pure Frankish blood by having African troops serving in their army. Unbeknownst to most of the world, nearly a million Africans fought on the side of the colonial powers in the war against the fascist regimes of Mussolini, Hitler, and Japan's Hirohito. British West Africa provided a large number of soldiers for campaigns within and outside of Africa. Over 240,000 soldiers from British West Africa fought, and tens of thousands of laborers, drivers, and carriers supported the British military efforts. In Asia, they participated in the Burma campaign.

Between the date of the armistice in June 1940 and the summer of 1944, when France was liberated, Africans constituted one of the main forces of the rank and file of the Free French military of General de Gaulle. The Free French capital was provisionally based in Algiers. For a time, French West Africa and French Equatorial Africa were on opposite sides of the war, with the former going with Vichy and the latter siding with de Gaulle. On the other side, under the Vichy in French West Africa, the number of African troops increased from fifty thousand to one hundred thousand. After the Allied victory in the North African campaign, these numbers were increased once again under the Free French.

Africans were also aware of the threat posed by the Nazis. For example, Germany had colonized both Tanganyika and Togo. So, the Tanganyikans knew the brutal potential of the German Empire. In 1936, Hitler demanded the return of the German colonies taken in the aftermath of their defeat in World War I. The Tanganyika League was created in 1938 with the purpose of resisting the resumption of German rule. Both European settlers and Africans were united in their opposition to Nazi rule. Over eighty-seven thousand Tanganyikans served the Allies in World War II.[9]

AFRICAN POST-WAR RESPONSE TO COLONIALISM

African participation in World War II occurred under the shadow of colonialism. Africans were being asked to fight for a democracy they did not have. Remembering this helps us understand the great sacrifice these soldiers made in the fight for European democracy. It also shows us how colonialism was anti-democratic.

Charles Menson, World War II veteran and a civil servant before and after Ghanaian independence, helped me understand the modern implications of this old relationship by summarizing life under British colonialism:

> Well, it was a question of master and servant. And then when the British came in, they assumed responsibility for the government of the country. So this is how the relationship came about. There was that big gap between the countrymen and the foreigners who came to take over the reins of government. And so we were more or less subjugated. But gradually things started to change when some of us were trained both in the States and in England. And then ideas started to come for a change to take place in this country.

K. B. Asante, also a civil servant before and after Ghanaian independence who served as Ghanaian leader Kwame Nkrumah's personal assistant, shared his views of growing up in the British colony of the Gold Coast and colonialism.

> Well, I didn't think it was anything special. Now, in those days we simply regarded the colonial regime as normal. Later on when I grew up, I found a few politicians who were questioning their presence here and what colonialism was all about. But when I was young, it was just a thing, and the aim was in many ways to be like the European, like the colonialists. It's as simple as that.
>
> I think it was in London I found the colonialism ideas existed really in the so-called mother country. I found that the British were not, they didn't know much about the so-called colonies. They didn't think . . . many of them did not think much of us. Generally speaking you found that you were not regarded as normal. For example, when I sat in a bus and nobody sat by me, I got used to it, because I could put my coat and books near me, and nobody bothered me. But little things like this, you find that you are not regarded as a normal human being.

African laborers under European colonialism, circa 1930. Screenshot from *African Independence*.

K. B. Asante, Ghanaian diplomat, who served as assistant to Kwame Nkrumah, at his home in Accra, Ghana, 2011. Screenshot from *African Independence*.

These insults of everyday life, which culminated in blatant discrimination and were codified into laws that separated racial groups, led to protest by the people in most European colonies in Africa. To better understand this response to colonialism, I sat down with one of the founding members of the African independence movement, His Excellency Kenneth Kaunda, president of Zambia from 1961 to 1991. He was also one of the founding

Charles Menson, Ghanaian veteran from World War II, before interview in Accra, Ghana, 2011. Screenshot from *African Independence*.

members of the liberation movement in Southern Africa. When I asked him to share how his life was impacted by colonialism, he replied,

> My father was a reverend in the Church of Scotland. He was sent from a country called Malawi today, and he was sent over in 1904 to Northern Rhodesia, Zambia today. I was brought up believing love God, your creator, with all your heart, all your soul, all your mind, all your strength. How do you relate to those He has made in His image, like you? The message, the commandment, was love thy neighbor as thou lovest thyself. This neighbor is not looked at in terms of color. Not in terms of tribe. Not even in terms of religion. I grew up in that atmosphere. There was a lot of discrimination, no doubt, in the country at that time. And because of that, I grew up as one of those rejecting, objecting, objecting strongly to discrimination in terms of color.

His Excellency Kenneth Kaunda before Zambian independence at a meeting on African independence in London, 1960. Screenshot from *African Independence*.

This was the case in East Africa as well, as Eloise Mukami Kimathi, freedom fighter against colonial rule in Kenya, reveals when discussing the motivation to fight against British colonialism,

> They saw I was black, and they thought I was something contemptuous and disgusting. That made us so annoyed because the colonial government thought they were closer to God, yet the same God was theirs and ours.

Some Africans saw the war effort as an opportunity to also advance rights on the colonial home front. Menson explained to me how participation in the war changed the people in the then so-called Gold Coast.

> I was in school then, and even at that time, they came to talk to us about military service. We were even hoping that they would recruit us into the army. So on the 24th of October 1941, I entered the army. Most of the people who joined the army were not tradesmen. They were not trained. So we trained them. In fact, all the troops that went to overseas, we were responsible for training them. But I was involved in moving troops from [Accra] to Ouagadougou and down to meet the Vichy government in Dakar.

Interview with Eloise Mukami Kimathi, freedom fighter and widow of the Kenyan Mau Mau leader Dedan Kimathi, at her home in 2008. Screenshot from *African Independence*.

Africans fought for the colonial power that controlled the area in which they lived. Nazi Germany criticized the British and the French for their use of Africans in war, and the Italians even satirized the United States for sending African Americans to fight. Yet both Italy and Vichy France employed African troops. At the end of the day, both sides sought to use black bodies to preserve or extend African colonialism. And at the end of World War II, white war veterans were rewarded with African land in Southern Africa, while black war veterans were left to fend for themselves, creating a system that contributed to persistent poverty and inequality in the Southern African region.

A young man when World War II occurred, His Excellency President Kenneth Kaunda explained to me how many Africans viewed the war as a European conflict:

> We did not think—although we had many young Zambians, Northern Rhodesians in those days, recruited by the colonial office—we did not think it was our war at all. We hated war. We hated exploitation. We hated all forms of human ridicule, God's child ridiculed, God's child hated, God's child destroyed because of color.

The Second World War, then, allowed the white world to see the contradictions of colonialism in a comparative perspective, that is, European colonialism in comparison to the mobilization of the modern European state to exploit other European states. While Britain spent as much as half its gross national product on the war effort, Nazi Germany fought the war by ransacking the economies of its victims in Belgium, Bohemia and Moravia, France, Norway, the Netherlands, and Poland. Their natural resources, infrastructures and populations were exploited to service the German war effort in their own countries and in Germany. This strategy was so successful that German citizens did not begin to feel the impact of the wartime shortages until 1944. In more ways than one, these policies of occupation mirrored European policies of colonialism and transformed the European political landscape.[10]

Wars of occupation were not unknown in Africa, of course. Far from new, African memories of wars against European colonial occupation were fresh. Well into the 1930s, African anti-colonial activities persisted. But there was a new awakening to and intensity of anti-colonial feelings following African participation in World War II. In part this was because of Africans' role in the war against fascism. But there was also the distinctive fascist attitude toward African populations in particular and subject populations in general.

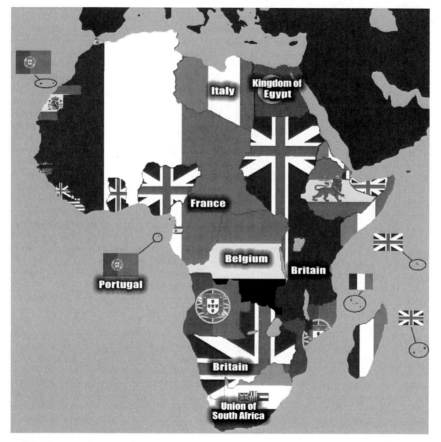

Political Map of 1930 Africa

Africa did not survive the war unscathed. While ruined cities were the most photogenic evidence of the devastation of Europe, African underdevelopment was evident to the world before and after the war. It took a war to create millions of homeless people in Europe (almost fifty million in the Soviet Union and Germany alone). It took a world war to seriously disrupt Western European transportation and communication and to produce economic, social, and political collapse to an extent unparalleled in modern European history. In every country occupied by Nazi forces, factories, land, machinery, and industrial products were expropriated without compensation. Financial institutions were seized to support the German war on the world.

Africa's inferior communication and transportation systems were a result of years of underdevelopment by European colonial powers before the start of World War II. From the very beginning of colonialism, the financial institutions of Africa had been reorganized by governments and corporations in Belgium, Britain, France, Portugal, Italy, and Germany to support and maintain the colonial administrations. This reorganization of African institutions was not done to develop infrastructure, improve education, or otherwise enhance the quality of life for African populations. The hypocrisy of the colonial mission of "African development" was made evident by the war, and confirmed by the rise of US influence, the Atlantic Charter, the United Nations, and new African activism. Yet the same European powers that Africa helped liberate during the war fought to maintain their colonies during the peace that came after.

AFRICAN POST-WAR UPRISINGS

The Arab nationalists in Algeria presented their moderate manifesto in the wake of the Allied landings in North Africa in February 1943. They emphasized their loyalty to France in this 1943 manifesto. The settler minority community considered independence under Arab and Berber majority populations unacceptable. French politicians continued to ignore the grievous injustices practiced by the colonial government. Even moderate Algerian nationalists, such as Ferhat Abbas, had their modest calls for self-government ignored by the French. They had submitted their manifesto when the Allies were on the offensive, having won a decisive victory for democracy and freedom on African land. Their cries for freedom and justice went unheard even after France was liberated. In 1944, the provisional head of the Free French, General de Gaulle, attempted political dialogue with the offer of voting rights to sixty-five thousand Muslim officers, graduates, and civil servants. These efforts turned out to be too little too late. Liberated France, it seems, was indifferent to the Algerian nationalists through the end of World War II. And then in May 1945—the very same month that Germany surrendered unconditionally—Algerians protested in the Kabylia region east of Algiers. The demonstrators gathered to protest French colonialism. In response, the French army reportedly massacred en masse forty-five thousand Algerian demonstrators.

A similar French response was given in Dakar, Senegal—headquarters of the territories of French West Africa. By the end of the summer of 1944, General de Gaulle was totally dependent on the United States for supplies and equipment for his army as the retreating Germans destroyed the French economy and much of its infrastructure. President Roosevelt had to reconcile the demands for war material from the US army fighting in Europe and Asia with requests for aid from Britain and the Soviets in the East. So President Roosevelt set the upper limits of the Free French forces at 250,000 men. De Gaulle integrated new French forces into his army by relieving African soldiers from their frontline positions. The Africans were asked to relinquish their weapons and the very uniforms they were wearing. These courageous men were sent south to spend the winter waiting for ships to take them home. In the south they suffered from shortages of food, clothing, and shelter, as did the civilian population.

All of this was happening in the shadow of one of the most important victories on the planet. Europe was devastated by the war, and Britain and France were reduced to rubble. Yet the Allies won the war. Under the leadership of the combined forces of the United States, Britain, France, and the Soviet Union, the Allies were victorious. Three months later, the United States dropped atomic bombs on the Japanese cities of Hiroshima and Nagasaki. Faced with total destruction, Emperor Hirohito (posthumously named Emperor Shōwa) admitted Japan's defeat and sued for peace.

The end of the Second World War and the nuclear devastation of Japan raised questions in the West about the continuation of colonialism. Nothing highlights this more than First Lady Eleanor Roosevelt, the first chair of the United Nations Commission on Human Rights and the overseer of the drafting of the Universal Declaration of Human Rights. In her statement to the United Nations General Assembly on the Universal Declaration of Human Rights in December 1948, she placed human rights in context:

> Man's desire for peace lies behind this declaration. The realization that
> the flagrant violation of human rights by Nazi and Fascist countries

Allied soldiers reading about the surrender of Germany, circa 1945. Screenshot from *African Independence*.

Polish refugees following World War II, 1945. Screenshot from *African Independence*.

Polish ruins during World War II, circa 1945. Screenshot from *African Independence*.

sowed the seeds of the last World War has supplied the impetus for the work. Man must have freedom in which to develop his full stature and through common effort to raise the level of human dignity.

In those countries occupied by Nazi Germany, repression, exploitation, and extermination became commonplace. The Nazi soldiers, storm troopers, and policemen disposed of the daily lives and very existence of tens of millions of people. The populations under the rule of the Reich were either put to the service of the German cause or killed. This was a new experience for Europeans. In the colonies, European states habitually disfranchised, indentured, and did great harm to the African population for their own benefit.[11] The European empires often used torture, rape, mutilation, and mass murder to coerce obedience to colonial authority. In Europe, these practices were largely unknown among Europeans themselves west of the Bug and Prut rivers. After World War II, Europeans had a better understanding of what colonial occupation felt like.

Many believe that if Hitler had won, Africa would have been parceled out between Germany and Italy. The people of Africa would have been subject to a system resembling slavery. The evidence for this is found in the fact that Nazi Germany fought the war in part by ransacking the

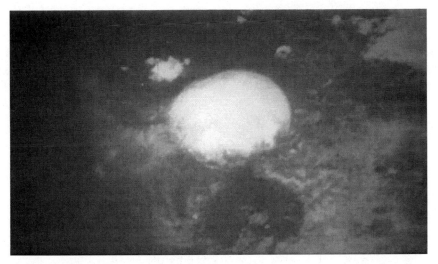

Atomic bomb mushroom looms over Hiroshima in Japan, 1945. Screenshot from *African Independence.*

Former First Lady Eleanor Roosevelt addressing the United Nations on the Universal Declaration of Human Rights, 1948. Screenshot from *African Independence.*

economies of its victims and mistreating their people.[12] The colonial powers, like Belgium and France, made significant involuntary contributions to the German war effort. Their factories, farms, and transportation systems were redirected to help the German war effort. By 1944, over 20 percent of the German labor force was composed of foreigners, and most of them were forced to work.

After the end of the war, the only "recognized" independent nations on the African continent were Ethiopia, Liberia, and the Union of South Africa. Liberia continued to be dominated by the elite with immigrant heritage, who claimed a culture and history that linked them to the United States.[13] Ethiopia had just suffered greatly under the yoke of the Italian invasion. And the Union of South Africa was brutally ruled by an elite with immigrant heritage who claimed a culture and history that linked them to Europe and the West. However, African soldiers returned from the war after seeing freedoms that they didn't experience in their own countries and witnessing Europeans as their equals on the battlefield. Many leveraged their military service to improve their lives. Menson describes life in Ghana after fighting for the British during World War II:

> Well, things had changed, because most of our people who went out to fight mixed up with other people from other countries, and the conception that obtained before of the blacks and the whites. . . . By the time our people came back, they had got a different picture of the world. And they had also entered into other areas of discipline, of training, and so on. They became better qualified to do jobs for their own country.

Africans had fought with great courage and served as the backbone of the British and French army. At any rate, most Africans returned to the colonial regimes they had left, on a mission to fight for independence in Africa. Many hoped that independence would lead to democracy and freedom. Many decommissioned soldiers were ex–prisoners of war (POWs) or recently sent from the front. The gathering of such large numbers of discontented men led to several serious uprisings among the soldiers.

In December 1944, at a military camp on the outskirts of Dakar in Thiaroye, veterans confronted their French officers over their pay and benefits. The discharged soldiers had recently returned from France. The uprising occurred among over one thousand ex-POWs, who were some of the first soldiers repatriated back to Africa. The confrontation led to the deaths of thirty-five African soldiers and a large number of wounded. Thirty-four ex-POWS were arrested and tried as "mutineers." The veterans contacted Lamine Gueye—the Senegalese French-educated lawyer, future mayor of

Dakar, and leader of the Parti Socialiste Sénégalais—to lead their defense. All thirty-four men were convicted and sentenced to prison terms ranging from one to ten years. A general amnesty was issued in June 1947. By that time, however, five of the men had died in jail. Nothing tells this story better than Ousmane Sembene's classic film, *Camp de Thiaroye*.

In 1944, as a French "citizen" and like many young Africans of his generation, Sembene was called to active duty to liberate France from German occupation. He was sent to the colony of Niger as a chauffeur in the Sixth Colonial Infantry Unit. In 1988, Sembene used film to tell a story that is rarely recorded in history books. This film presents soldiers from all over Africa who fought with the French army and who were sent to Thiaroye expecting, like all other veterans, their demobilization, bonuses, and severance pay. But at the end of 1944, the French command decided to cheat the Africans out of their severance, provoking a mutiny among the veterans. Showing no mercy, let alone gratitude for the years of African help, the French military establishment responded with an overwhelming armored attack that killed many of the African soldiers in the camp. Camp de Thiaroye captures the symbolism of the attitude of the colonial powers regarding African efforts to extend the freedom and democracy they fought for in the Second World War. Sembene's film captures the African indignation toward the brutal repression of former prisoners of war whose only crime was to claim money that was theirs. Similar African uprisings occurred in France in Côte d'Azur (known as the French Riviera), Saint-Raphaël, and Antibes. All of these uprisings reflected the change in the soldiers' attitude toward French authority and colonial ideas.

African soldiers were cheated and even murdered by the very army they fought for during World War II. The French used the same tactics that the Germans used during their occupation of other European states. In exchange for contributing to the war effort, France had promised the Africans independence. In February of 1944, de Gaulle made clear his vision of colonial Africa in the post-war period:

> In French Africa, as in every land where men live under our flag, there can be no true progress unless men are able to benefit from it morally and materially on their native soil, unless they can raise themselves little by little to a level where they can partake in the management of their own affairs. It is the duty of France to bring this about.

Once victorious, however, France soon reneged on its war promises. And while the day of Germany's surrender was celebrated worldwide as

"Victory Day," in most of Africa it symbolized a return to colonial rule and the status quo.

The African colonies had helped the Allies defeat the German war of occupation, exploitation, and repression in which Nazi soldiers and policemen disrupted the lives of millions of European citizens. North Africa provided several hundred thousand men, including over one hundred thousand Algerians. African soldiers in the Tirailleurs Sénégalais took part in the liberation of France in Corsica (between September and October of 1943), the Italian campaign (June 15, 1944), and the Provence campaign (August 1944) and joined with the main body of the French army. Yet the French troops were led by General de Gaulle in their victorious march beneath L'Arc de Triomphe in Paris, with the masses of Parisians lining the boulevards and French women kissing the victorious soldiers. At the same time, French troops in Africa were massacring the protesting Algerians and putting down "mutinies" in Senegal. World War II produced different realities—one that offered the hope of freedom, liberation, and reconstruction in Europe and the United States, while the cloud of colonialism and repression in Asia and Africa mired the others. Indeed, these realities were different sides of the same coin.[14]

Having fought a desperate war for Europeans against European imperialism run amok, African soldiers were now returning home inevitably inspired by the victory of freedom, democracy, and independence over Nazi tyranny. And just as inevitably, many Africans now wanted those very same liberties for themselves. That meant going head to head with the very same European powers for which they had recently fought. And in October of 1945, only five months after the end of the war, Africans from across the continent—and even some from as far away as America—made the historic trek to Manchester, England, that would become known as the Fifth Pan-African Congress. They had come to declare their desire for freedom in the very heart of the Europe that had dominated them, yet which still held the key to their liberty. They knew all too well that Europe placed little value on African life. The myth of civilized Europe and barbaric Africa was unraveling.

FIFTH PAN-AFRICAN CONGRESS

Calls for recognizing Africa's humanity on the international front were fortified by the efforts of the Pan-African movement. In 1944 the National Association for the Advancement of Colored People (NAACP) asked founder W. E. B. Du Bois to return to the organization. Born in the United States three years after the end of slavery, Du Bois, the great African American savant, the first African American to earn a PhD from Harvard University, founder of the NAACP and the civil rights movement, and the father of Pan-Africanism, organized a number of Pan-African Congresses dating back to 1900. He was forced to retire from his professorship at Atlanta University by the university president in 1939. In 1944, at age seventy-five, he returned to the NAACP as director of special research.

Under Du Bois's leadership, a first Pan-African Congress was held in Paris, France, in February 1919 in the Grand Hotel, Boulevard des Capucines. Presided over by Blaise Diagne of Senegal and Du Bois, fifty-seven delegates attended the congress from different parts of the world. The chairman of the Foreign Affairs Committee represented France; Belgium sent a member of its Peace Delegation; former minister of foreign affairs, Friere d'Andrade, represented Portugal; and the United States sent William E. Walling and Charles Edward Russell. Resolutions passed at the gathering called for another congress and made demands for people of African ancestry. The congress members called for the internationalization of the former German colonies in Africa. Toward the end of the congress, Du Bois, as the principal organizer, promised to convene another congress two years later. The congress submitted a petition that Du Bois delivered to both the League of Nations and the Peace Conference that was simultaneously meeting in Paris.

The Second Congress was assembled and held in London, Brussels, and Paris in August and September 1921. This congress was much larger than its predecessor, with forty-one delegates from Africa, thirty-five from the United States, twenty-four from Europe, and seven from the West Indies. This congress was quite similar to the other in intent; however, more radical resolutions were adopted. Resolutions criticized the colonial system and racism; asked that the sovereignty of Abyssinia, Haiti, and Liberia be respected; and challenged the world to recognize the absolute equality of all men and women regardless of race.

The next two congresses were relatively uneventful. The 1923 congress was held in London and Lisbon. The meetings were small and disorganized. Four years later, in 1927, a distinguished group of African American women organized another Pan-African Congress in New York. There were over two hundred delegates representing twenty-two American states and ten other countries. Once again, only a few individuals living on the African continent were present at the meeting. However, it is important to recognize that African American women were the conveners of the 1927 congress.

The majority of delegates at the first four congresses were intellectuals from Europe and America. Du Bois recognized this dynamic: "So far, the Pan-African idea was still American rather than African." This was to change with the onset of World War II. The Italian invasion of Ethiopia had a profound influence on the development of Pan-Africanism and the ideal of African independence. Every element of the Pan-African movement joined the battle cry for Ethiopia to be returned to Ethiopians. Marcus Garvey's Universal Negro Improvement Association (UNIA) and the Du Boisian wings of the Pan-African movement were in agreement on this essential issue. The invasion of Ethiopia catalyzed and united Africans in the diaspora. Members of every branch of the movement stood together in support of the return of Ethiopia to independence. These same individuals would breathe a fresh and new life into the Pan-African movement. This new vigor resulted in the 1945 Pan-African Congress.[15]

Amy Jacques Garvey, the widow of Marcus Garvey and a strong critic of the Italian occupation of Ethiopia, expressed her deep concern about the direction of Pan-Africanism following the impending end of the war. She took action and rallied interest in the Fifth Pan-African Congress. Unlike all the previous congresses, the fifth one would unite the intellectual movement of the Du Boisian–led congresses, the growing trade union movements based on the African continent, and the grassroots efforts of the Universal Negro Improvement Association. In 1944, Du Bois, George Padmore, Kwame Nkrumah, and others joined Mrs. Garvey calling for a Pan-African Congress to be held in Europe as soon as possible after the war.

George Padmore was one of the first Pan-African diplomats. He was a lawyer from Trinidad who studied in the United States. His involvement with the Workers Party, the Communist Party, and the American Negro Labor Congress led to his being based in Moscow as the head of the Negro Bureau of the Red International of Labor Unions. He was a strong proponent of black labor organizations around the world. This history was enough to lead to his being barred from returning to the United States. In the 1930s he became an important Pan-African supporter of the African independence movement. With his longtime friend C. L. R. James he became one of the leading African and Caribbean intellectuals fighting colonialism. When Nkrumah arrived in London to study law, it was Padmore who met him at the station. Padmore had already begun the work to organize the Fifth Pan-African Congress in Manchester at this time. Following this career trajectory, he would become an important factor in the period before and after independence in African nations. He, like Frantz

Fanon in Algeria, would have an opportunity to officially represent the newly independent African nation of Ghana.

Founded by Marcus Garvey, the UNIA was one of the most important advocates of African independence in the post–World War I period. Five years before the end of World War II, Garvey died in obscurity, with his organization only a shadow of the promise it showed in the early 1900s. On April 4, 1944, Amy Jacques Garvey continued the work of the UNIA and contacted Du Bois about writing what she called the "African Freedom Charter" as a way of amplifying the promises of the Atlantic Charter, signed in 1941 and later ratified by the Allied nations fighting against fascism. Mrs. Garvey challenged Du Bois to convene a conversation that would focus on the needs of freedom and independence on the African continent. In reply, Du Bois contacted Paul Robeson and others about convening another Pan-African Congress.

On March 19, 1945, George Padmore published a call for the Fifth Pan-African Congress to convene once World War II had ended. As the dust settled, the conversation about the Fifth Pan-African Congress intensified. A heated discussion took place between Du Bois and Padmore about how to proceed. Working quietly in the background, with full knowledge of African participation in World War II, were leaders from Africa living in Europe. These African freedom fighters included Malawi's Hastings Banda, Nigeria's Obafemi Awolowo, Trinidad's Padmore, Kenya's Jomo Kenyatta, and Ghana's Nkrumah. Under the leadership of Nkrumah and Padmore, the vision of Du Bois was rebirthed, and Africans, for the first time, both initiated and led the Pan-African Congress. Nkrumah became the leading voice and, following the Pan-African Congress, founded, with Kenyatta, the Pan-African Federation. Along with the West African Students' Union, this federation would become an essential voice in the demand for more rights for Africans in the political process on the African continent.

Under the banner of the NAACP, Du Bois organized a Conference on Colonialism. A precursor to the Fifth Pan-African Congress, it was held on April 6, 1945, in Harlem. Many Africans, including none other than Nkrumah, attended the conference. Born in the British Gold Coast colony, young Nkrumah attended Lincoln University and the University of Pennsylvania. While in the United States, he worked on the docks of the Delaware River, wrote anti-colonial articles, and engaged in political struggle and debate around the future of Africa. When he traveled to London, Nkrumah became the visionary force behind the Pan-African Congress convened in 1945. He elevated the conversation among Padmore, Amy Jacques Garvey, and Du Bois into a process of action.[16]

The World Federation of Trade Unions (WFTU) also played a key role in the Fifth Pan-African Congress. The organization had met in London in February 1945 to discuss the global organization of labor. In attendance at the meeting were representatives from Africa, the Caribbean, and individuals and organizations that represented African descendants living in London, Lancashire, Liverpool, and Manchester. Seizing the moment, the Pan-Africanists in attendance called for assembling the colonial delegates at another meeting to discuss Pan-African issues. The delegates met in Manchester in March, and there it was decided that the Fifth Pan-African Congress would be held when the next WFTU meeting was set to take place, September 25 to October 9 of that year, in Paris. An agenda was set, and rapporteurs were appointed in preparation for the coming congress. A "Special International Conference Secretariat" was assigned the task of making all the necessary preparations. Along with Padmore and Nkrumah (who served as joint secretaries) and Kenyatta (who served as assistant secretary), the secretariat consisted of Peter Milliard from British Guiana (chairman), T. R. Makonnen from Ethiopia (treasurer), and Peter Abrahams from South Africa (publicity secretary). The agenda was approved, and most trade unions, cooperatives, and other progressive organizations in the colonial English-speaking West Indies and Africa endorsed the agenda and pledged to send delegates. When time was too short or distance prevented sending representatives, the organizations gave mandates to individuals traveling to Paris for the WFTU meeting or they appointed representatives in Britain.[17]

Around the same time, the United Nations and several other organizations were being discussed and created. The League of Nations' inability to prevent World War II marked its death. The demise of the League facilitated the Bretton Woods Monetary and Financial Conference in New Hampshire and the Dumbarton Oaks Conference in Washington, D.C., in 1944.[18] The Bretton Woods Conference was held to establish one of the first internationally negotiated world systems to govern monetary relations and regulate commercial and financial markets among independent nations. Given the needs of the Marshall Plan and other regulatory systems, the Bretton Woods Conference would come to symbolize the modern capitalist world. It was in this context that the International Monetary Fund and the World Bank were created.

On the political and military side, the Dumbarton Oaks Conference was convened to stop future world wars by organizing the most powerful nations on earth to oppose such aggression. The essential idea was that an organization, under the leadership of a Security Council, could ensure peace in the future. This key element of a Security Council was to be a major component of what would become the United Nations.

Less than twenty days after the NAACP conference on colonialism, the United Nations Conference on International Organization was born in 1945 in San Francisco. Du Bois added his voice to this meeting with the colonial question and the future independence of Africa. He raised grave concerns about the creation of the Security Council. Du Bois thought the efforts to replace the League of Nations with a better federation was wise and honorable. He saw the founding of the United Nations conferences in 1944 as an essential step in ensuring peace and restoring civilization. Yet he voiced concern that the failure to emphasize the rights of the colonial peoples, as well as the establishment of a Security Council dominated by the most powerful states, would result in recurrent wars.[19]

The site of the Fifth Pan-African Congress, Chorlton Town Hall, served the area of Chorlton-on-Medlock, then known as Chorlton Row until it was incorporated into the city of Manchester in 1838. The word "Chorlton" means freemen. Hidden from view but flowing through the district is the River Medlock, from which the name derived. Architect Richard Lane designed Chorlton Town Hall, with its Doric columns reflecting the classical styles favored at the time before Victorian Gothic became the style of the day.

On the building's facade, a red plaque bears the City of Manchester's coat of arms, with the words "Fifth Pan-African Conference was held here 15th–21st October 1945. Decisions taken at this conference led to the liberation of African countries." Underneath, a rectangular red plaque lists the names of some of the principal participants in the conference, with the words "Participants in that historic event included Ras Makonnen, Kwame Nkrumah, Jomo Kenyatta, Amy Garvey, W. E. B. Du Bois, George Padmore."

The mills of Chorlton, which catapulted the small village into the urban space it has become, were built during the Industrial Revolution. The unscrupulous mill owners and landlords provided filthy slum houses back to back to accommodate the flood of people who came to work in the new textile factories in the early 1900s. Most of the mainly Irish workers who lived there were poor and worked in the mills.

That African independence was a reality somewhere in the world meant that colonialism could not be justified. It was as if this celebration of African independence at the Fifth Pan-African Congress was to remind all in attendance that African independence already existed and that Africans bore witness to European civilization's barbarism in their everyday lives.

The inspirational and beautiful words of Eleanor Roosevelt on the eve of the Universal Declaration of Human Rights demonstrate the coming together of the African independence movement, the racial hypocrisy of the Nazi doctrine, and the birth of a new commitment to human progress in the name of human rights. Africans participated in raising the flag of liberation all over Europe in the name of democracy and freedom. Why not do the same for Africa?

The people of Africa and the continent's diaspora began a march toward independence and social justice. The Second World War had raised the stakes. It was at this historic Pan-African Congress held in 1945 that Africans considered a movement that would attempt to sever once and for all the bonds that tied Africa to its colonizers. It was here that Africans also attempted to put an end to their continent's second-class status in the world. Here in Manchester, the African independence movement would dare to imagine a bold new African dream of self-determination and sovereignty.

The Fifth Pan-African Congress convened with some two hundred delegates representing Africa and the continent's descendants the world over. At the congress, Padmore introduced Du Bois as the "father of Pan-Africanism." With deference due to his earlier efforts as a founding member of the movement, Du Bois was confirmed as the presiding international chairman during the conference, and he and Peter Milliard, president of the Negro Association of Manchester and the chairman of the British section of the movement, occupied the chair jointly. Amy Jacques Garvey represented the UNIA. In attendance at this meeting were people from Europe and the Americas from varied walks of life, with a fraternal delegate here and there and observers from the non-African world. Several trade unions and cultural and political organizations were represented. The African contingent was significantly represented. These Africans would take the message back to every corner of the continent and light the fire of independence. South Africa's Peter Abrahams would later observe, "This Congress, therefore, was the most representative yet assembled by Africans and peoples of African descent to plan and work for the liquidation of Imperialism."[20]

The conference fanned the flames of independence. I sat down with the second president of Tanzania, His Excellency Ali Hassan Mwinyi, a freedom fighter in his own right, to add some context about the significance of the Fifth Pan-African Congress for the African continent. Here is what he had to say:

> Well, here you are. Now, the Africans in Africa have realized the need
> for independence, independence of Africans, the whole Africa, now

Interview with the second president of Tanzania, Ali Hassan Mwinyi, at his official residence in Dar es Salaam, Tanzania, 2010. Screenshot from *African Independence*.

Ghana had started. Mwalimu Nyerere had started something here. And at that time, even some leaders of Zanzibar had started this idea. Yes. It was just like a fire, a bushfire spreading.

The independence movement in Africa grew directly out of this past. A new way of thinking was sweeping across the continent. A new movement was giving birth to ideas once only dreamed of by African leaders in the past.

2

THE END OF COLONIAL RULE
Beginnings of Independence

The changes following the end of the war required a new view of the future. The option to ignore these changes in the world and press on, as colonial subjects like before, like an ostrich, had its impossible attractions. The fading sentimentality of a nostalgic past is usually an unworkable and far less interesting option, especially for men and women who have gained a more enlightened and international view of the world. The Second World War and the presence of a new generation of intellectuals and a rising middle class with political aspirations had an impact on the future course of Africa in its relationship with the world. There were major changes in the world after World War II, at the beginning of the Cold War, but it was in this new world order that the story of the movement for African independence accelerated.

As we investigate what independence means to different people and see how it manifests itself in different ways across Africa, we will examine what happened to all the great aspirations of the Pan-African Congress. We identify the new leaders, along with their struggles and dreams for their new nations and for a liberated continent. We document the links between different independence movements and meet some of the key African figures that helped to make it all happen. We look at why the United States and Russia demanded that France and Britain decolonize after the war and how Kwame Nkrumah, organizer of the 1945 Pan-African Congress, became the symbol of African independence.

Nkrumah led Ghana to independence from Britain in 1957. From Ghana, African and global forces came together in support of African independence to such an extent that the United Nations (UN) declared 1960 the year of Africa. Over twenty-three new nations joined the UN from Africa. As the drive for freedom and self-rule accelerated, Africa seemed ready to enter a golden age where everything was possible. But after a few years, these nascent movements faltered as the Cold War turned the dream of African independence into a nightmare.

THE MOVEMENT MATERIALIZES

I do not want to be misunderstood. The fight against colonial injustices did not begin after World War II. Demands for change on the African continent were not new. Long before World War II, African leaders had demanded more political rights.

In the 1920s, the National Congress of British West Africa secured a say in the election of the colonial legislative councils of Nigeria, the Gold Coast Colony, Sierra Leone, and Gambia. The South Africa Native National Congress was created in 1912 and became the African National Congress (ANC) in 1923. After World War I, Tanzania was administered via a League of Nations mandate under the Belgians, the Portuguese, and the British. In French West Africa, the Quartres Communes had citizenship rights. The Egyptian king was the official head of self-government under British protection. France governed each of its colonies as part of *la plus grande* France, and, for example, the franchise in African colonies translated into a higher number of African representatives in the French parliament. These are all examples of political gains for Africans that took place before the accelerated movement for independence got started.

In 1914, Blaise Diagne of Senegal was elected the first African deputy member of the French National Assembly. He eventually became a junior minister. In the post-war period, the number of African deputies in the French legislature was raised to twenty-four. Diagne also played a critical role in convening the 1919 Pan-African Congress with W. E. B. Du Bois. In 1934, Diagne's successor was Galandou Diouf, a political leader who ran the main political organization in Dakar. In the post-war period, each territory got a local assembly, and a "federal" assembly was set up for the two regions of French West Africa and French Equatorial Africa.[1] The political context was changing in Africa, and these changes had implications for events yet to take place in Europe.

When the Second World War was over, Western Europe was hard pressed to govern and feed its own people. Nazi Germany had transformed Western Europe into underdeveloped nations, while the same war had transformed the United States into the leading developed nation. The collapse of Europe following World War II astonished the world and revealed a shift in the balance of power from Europe to the United States.[2]

In the aftermath of the war, Europe was in misery and desolation. Newsreels of the time show a stream of helpless civilians trekking through a blasted landscape of slum-like, war-worn battlefields. Shaven-headed concentration camp inmates along with orphaned children wandered about staring listlessly into the camera. Starvation and disease were everywhere. The most visual evidence of the devastation of the war was the ruined cities. They came to serve as a universal symbol of the implosion of European civilization in the twentieth century. The visual evidence of this international tragedy led the United Nations to ratify a Universal Declaration of Human Rights. Never again could people be treated in such an inhumane manner without facing the wrath of the nations of the world. The images from the newsreels have etched into our memory the devastation of postwar Europe.

Despite having been decimated by the war, Europe continued to colonize most of Africa and Asia. For Britain and France, in particular, the colonies demonstrated their value in the war as vital sources of human and material resources, which were decisive in their battles with Italy, Germany, and Japan.

The cost of maintaining an empire in Africa rose during the Second World War, and this became particularly obvious to the two largest colonial powers, Britain and France. In the aftermath of the war, economic disruption and displacement made maintaining an empire even more difficult, although the material value of the colonies was still considerable. The cost of policing, servicing, administering, and soldiering had all gone up during the war. The British, French, and Portuguese found their most fervent support among settler classes of entrepreneurs, farmers, and ranchers in places like Algeria, Kenya, Southern Rhodesia, the Belgian Congo, Guinea-Bissau, Cape Verde, Mozambique, and Angola.[3]

Portugal was the smallest and poorest colonial power. Portuguese colonies in Angola and Mozambique provided raw materials at favorable prices and a restricted and captive market for Portuguese exports. Spain had already lost most of its empire to Britain and to her own settlers who demanded independence. The rise of the United States coincided with the death of Spain as a major colonial power. After the war, the only Spanish colonies in Africa were the small enclaves in Spanish Sahara, adjacent to Morocco, and Spanish Guinea, located between Cameroon and Gabon. Africa Orientale Italiana died with Italy's defeat in World War II.[4]

While the fate of Italian colonialism in Africa may have signaled what was to come, much of Africa remained in European hands immediately after the war. Most colonial powers expected the end of colonialism to be far off. The worldwide movement for independence had begun with the war's end. The cry for European powers to relinquish their colonial claims was getting louder and louder among the colonized. Declarations of independence in Asia, Africa, and among many anti-governmental forces in Latin America, and demands for civil rights and Black Power in the United States and Europe, all challenged the inhuman practices of colonialism.

African rejections of colonialism were comparable to European rejections of fascism. In post-war Europe, there was widespread hope for rapid social transformation, whereas in post-war Africa, the expectation was for social transformation to be *dramatic*. Many young men who stepped onto the battleground for Europe had known no other form of public life. Political parties were either banned or never heard of. To oppose the authorities was illegal. While this parallel between the anti-fascist and anti-colonial struggles may seem obvious to most today, it was not obvious to the colonial powers in the immediate post–World War II period.

Although post-war Europe was barely feeding its own people, they continued to rule Africa. Without access to the soil, supplies, and men of Africa, the British and French would have had to fight a very different war, and they may have been at a decisive disadvantage in their struggles against the fascist Axis of Italy, Germany, and Japan. Then, after the war, Britain and France needed their colonies' help to rebuild.

Much of Africa remained in European imperial hands, governed either directly from the imperial metropolis, through European settlers or an African governing class of European-trained leaders or intellectuals, or indirectly through indigenous rulers in alliance with European masters and interests. At first, post-war Europeans seemed unaware of the effect the fight against fascism had on the stability of colonial Africa. None of the colonial powers anticipated the immediate challenges that soon arose from their colonial subjects.[5]

World War II had changed everything, and a return to the old days of colonialism in any form was out of the question. This was obviously the view of the freedom fighters, but it was just as evident to the older generation of African colonial administrators. Additionally, the United States supported an end to the colonial monopolies of African and Asian economies by European empires. The United States had decisively ended World War II by dropping two atomic bombs on Japan. Every nation in the world now knew the United States had the most powerful military arsenal on the planet. This monopoly on nuclear weapons changed the global equation, and while the Soviets rushed to deploy their own nuclear devices, the US economy was booming. With its decisive weapons of mass destruction and strong dollar, the United States gained influence over the rest of the Western alliance.[6]

The first five post-war years were to prove crucial; many people at the time feared the worst in terms of Europe's resuscitation. The scale of the European chaos caused by the war seemed out of hand. Observers from Europe and elsewhere saw Europe spiraling out of control after the devastation caused by the war. Du Bois wrote, "We are face to face with the greatest tragedy that has ever overtaken the world. The collapse of Europe is to us the more astounding because of the boundless faith which we have had in European civilization."[7] General opinion maintained that the European continent would experience decades of poverty and possibly collapse back into fascism and civil war.[8]

In Asia, Britain had lost its East Asian colonies to Japan, having been forced to surrender Singapore in February 1942. The British military was able to prevent India from falling into Japanese hands, and they recovered all the lost territories after the defeat of Japan. Two years after the end of the war, India was politically independent from the British, and the sun had begun to set on the British flag.[9]

In the course of the first two years following the Allied victory—one forged with considerable African sacrifice—the mood of the continent swung from returning home victorious to growing disillusion in the face of Africa-wide inflation, strike waves, and political unrest. The development of Africa could only be accomplished with Western money and technology, along with a policy of political independence. Western Europe was lacking in both of these, so the new superpowers had to step up to the plate.

Before the end of World War II, a number of political demonstrations and strikes had taken place all over Africa. The most common demands were for reforms of the colonial system. Few people foresaw the growth of political parties demanding independence. In 1941, the Comité de l'Unité Togolaise was founded. In 1942, Nigerians created the Nigerian Reconstruction Group, and in the Sudan, the Ashiqqua (National Unionist Party) was established. In 1944, the Nyasaland National Congress (in Malawi) was founded. In the same year, so was the National Council of Nigeria. In 1945, it would be renamed the National Council of Nigeria and the Cameroons in recognition of the participation of Cameroonian groups. This was an eventful year, as the Arab League, founded in Cairo, issued the Arab Charter and, in the vein of the Pan-African Congress, called for Pan-Arab cultural, religious, linguistic, and political unity. The Rassemblement Democratique Africain (RDA), under the leadership of Félix Houphouët-Boigny, was also created out of a federation of the various organizations that had developed throughout the French colonies in West and Equatorial Africa. The following year, in 1946, the Northern Rhodesian African National Congress was founded.[10]

African elites formed study groups, trade unions, and political parties. In 1945, the same year as the congress in Manchester, the most important organizations in the French colonial territories were confederated under the RDA, which became the leading nationalist organization in the French colonial territories. Originally the RDA was associated with the Communist Party of France. In the 1950s, the RDA was split: the parliamentarians were led by Fèlix Houphouët-Boigny of the Ivory Coast, who served as the party's president, and the more radical socialists were led by the secretary general of the party, Gabriel d'Arboussier. The parliamentarians were so called because of their membership and influence in the French parliament.

In January 1944, Free French politicians and high-ranking colonial officials in the French African colonies met in Brazzaville, the capital of French Equatorial Africa. At this conference, they recommended social, political, and economic reforms in the administration of the colonies.

The Brazzaville Conference had a significant influence on the new constitution promulgated in France in 1946. The French constitution allowed French African citizens to send additional representatives and deputies to the French National Assembly. The radical socialists wanted to maintain a strong association between the RDA and the Communist Party of France. In the ensuing crisis, the parliamentarians in the RDA met separately and declared the end of the RDA's connections with the French Communist Party and fired d'Arboussier from his position as secretary general. Houphouët-Boigny and his colleagues declared a "tactical retreat" in which they abandoned "systematic opposition" to French colonialism and called for "constructive collaboration"

Several dissenting voices made themselves heard. They ranged from the Union of Peoples of the Cameroons (UPC), which had launched an armed rebellion against France in 1949, to the RDA in Niger under the leadership of Djibo Bakary. The dissenters were expelled from the RDA for not accepting the new policies. In 1948, Leopold Sedar Senghor founded the Bloc Démocratique Sénégalais.[11]

During the 1950s in the British colonial territories, several other movements were consolidated, as Africans were increasingly dissatisfied with their treatment by colonial powers and the white minority settler governments. During this time, the world witnessed the emergence or revival of numerous political organizations on the continent, including the Sierra Leone People's Party (1950), the Uganda National Congress (1952), the Tanganyika African National Union (1954), and the African National Congress in Southern Rhodesia (1957).

Strategically, the British military presence in Egypt was important for Britain's relations in the eastern Mediterranean and the rest of Africa, especially North Africa and the horn region. Following the end of World War II, the Egyptian government demanded a change in the agreement of "self-government" it had with the British. Negotiations between 1946 and 1950 failed, and Egyptian guerillas began fighting for independence against the British military in 1951. In 1952, popular anti-British protests accelerated with the destruction of British property in Cairo.[12]

Meanwhile, in the Sudan, three groups emerged after an elected Legislative Assembly was created in 1947. They were divided between those who wanted self-government and to preserve the link with Britain, those who wanted independence and a closer link with Egypt, and those who spoke for the southern population that was neither Arab nor Muslim. In 1952, following the revolution in Egypt, Britain and Egypt agreed to "prepare" Sudan for independence. By 1955, elections were held, and power was transferred to the Sudanese people. Sudan became a parliamentary republic in 1956. The British and Egyptian armed forces left the country. However, the future of Sudan continued to be complicated by the third force, the southerners, who were apprehensive about northern rule. Furthermore, as a model of what was to come in the post-independence years, two years after Sudan gained independence, General Ibrahim Abboud led a military coup in that country.[13]

The Italian colonies of Tripolitania, Cyrenaica, and Fezzan formed what we now know as Libya. After the fascist defeat, the area was occupied by British and French troops. Britain occupied Cyrenaica and Tripolitania. France administered Fezzan. In 1949, the UN resolved that Libya should attain independence as the United Kingdom of Libya. On December 24, 1951, Sayid Idris as-Sanusi, the emir of Cyrenaica, became the new nation's first King Idris.[14]

During and following World War II, social protest became a routine form of political participation. Changes in African political aspirations and shifts in the world political order presented new opportunities for social movements on the African continent in several colonial territories. These protests became increasingly nationalistic. The arguments for creating independent African nations became louder and louder. African leaders wanted a better future with inalienable freedoms, which Europeans regularly experienced because of their military and economic sacrifices. Participation in defeating the fascists and the new spirit of the post-war movement resulted in renewed calls for sovereignty and equality among Africans.[15]

These events were captured time and time again in newsreels from the BBC and other Western outlets as independence was achieved across the African continent. Faces of new leaders became iconic images representing the hope of a new Africa. These men and women presented themselves as people who could marshal in a new era of political, economic, and social change for Africa.

Britain was learning that a negotiated transfer of power would avoid armed conflict and that direct control was costly in financial and political terms. Yes, Ethiopia, Liberia, Morocco, Tunisia, Libya, Egypt, and the Sudan were independent; however, it was the transformation of the Gold Coast into Ghana that marked a shift in British policy regarding ending colonialism in Africa. Ethiopia and Liberia were independent long before World War II had begun. Morocco, Tunisia, Libya, Egypt, and the Sudan compose what is described as North Africa (including Algeria), and all declared independence following World War II in the 1950s. With the exception of Morocco, all deposed the monarchs who negotiated the first phase of their independence. In fact, a big difference between Morocco and the other countries may have been the relationships of colonial authorities and the traditional monarchs in these areas of Africa.

For example, the French socialist government of Guy Mollet proposed reforms and clearly wanted to compromise with the African independence movement. Mollet's efforts began in Morocco and Tunisia, where freedom fighters were among the first to take advantage of his new policies. In 1934 in Tunisia, Habib Bourguiba split with the Old Destour Party and formed the Neo-Destour Party. Bourguiba was a Paris-trained lawyer who founded the pro-independence militant newspaper *L'Action Tunisienne*. He was an important freedom fighter who worked to organize Tunisians for independence and became the country's first president, from 1957 to 1987.

Bourguiba accused the Old Destour Party leaders of being reactionary and was imprisoned several times for his efforts before World War II. In 1944, he moved to Cairo to avoid French repression. Soon thereafter, the French, bowing to the nationalists' pressures, reorganized the Council of Ministers and the Grand Council, an elected body with equal French and Tunisian representation. The freedom fighters responded by demanding independence.[16] Cairo's 1952 revolution was an important precursor for Ghana, Tanzania, and Zambia and was an important site of refuge for political leaders.

In 1949, Bourguiba returned to Tunisia from Egypt, and the next year the Neo-Destour Party sought a transfer of sovereignty and executive control to the Tunisian people. The French settlers represented about 10 percent of the population at that time, and they opposed all efforts toward independence. In 1952, Bourguiba and other leaders of the Neo-Destour Party were arrested in Tunisia. The freedom fighters actively resisted colonialism and engaged violently with some of the settlers. Represented by their own militaristic organization, called La Main Rouge ("Red Hand"), the settlers came close to civil war with Tunisia.

Bourguiba had been a strong supporter of the Free French during the war. The combined strength of his party and the newly formed trade union federation gave the Tunisian people leverage in demanding national independence and self-determination.

In March 1955, Tunisia was granted self-government by the French colonial authorities. The French retained control over foreign affairs, defense, and internal security. On March 20, 1956, France recognized the independence of Tunisia.

The Neo-Destour Party won ninety-eight seats in the legislature, and Bourguiba became prime minister on April 11. France maintained its base in Bizerta in order to facilitate its war with Algeria. France rejected the Bourguiba government's protests and efforts to broker a peace that would aid in Algerian independence.

In Morocco, the nationalist groups organized themselves into the Independence Party (Hizb al-Istiqlal) and began to work with the sultan, Muhammad V. Once a trade union federation was formed, Istiqlal dominated its politics and increased the call for independence. By 1953, the party and the sultan had grown closer, and the sultan demanded total sovereignty. In response, the sultan was deposed and exiled. The political agitation turned into forceful resistance to colonial rule, with the sultan as the unifying symbol of independence.

In response to this heightened struggle for independence, French policy changed. The new socialist government opened negotiations with the Neo-Destour Party in Tunisia and the sultan of Morocco. In March 1956, Mollet's government granted independence to Algeria's neighboring colonies of Morocco and Tunisia. In Morocco, both the international city of Tangier and the Spanish colony (also known as the Western Sahara) were incorporated into the new state. The sultan became king of Morocco in 1957.[17]

In the aftermath of World War II, Britain began to discuss self-government for its Sub-Saharan African colonies, having witnessed defeat at the hands of freedom fighters in Asia and North Africa. British leaders nevertheless believed that such an arrangement would arrive toward the end of the century. For reasons of self-interest, it gave lip service to major programs of development, agriculture, transportation, education, and health care for its colonial subjects. In reality it provided these developments only in circumstances in which European economic and political interests were primary, such as in South Africa, Kenya, and the then Southern Rhodesia. Nevertheless, universities were established or expanded in the Gold Coast, Nigeria, the Sudan, and Uganda.[18]

POLITICAL INDEPENDENCE IN GHANA

In the more "mature" colonies, Britain pursued a strategy of permitting Africans entry into the colonial administration. This is how Nkrumah got his start as leader of government business in the Gold Coast, which at that time was part of the British Empire. As a member of the colonial administration, the organizing secretary of the Fifth Pan-African Congress became the pioneer of the African independence movement.[19]

J. B. Danquah earned his doctorate at the University of London. He had written a book on Akan law and religion that was highly regarded in Britain. Danquah and other intellectuals and bureaucrats formed the United Gold Coast Convention (UGCC) under the slogan "Self-government in the shortest possible time." In order to build popular support for their movement, Danquah and his colleagues hired the young Nkrumah as a full-time organizer. The fiery Nkrumah returned home to Accra. Although it would take many long years for Nkrumah's dream of Ghanaian independence to come to fruition, Nkrumah hit the ground running. He returned from studying in the United States and England and spearheaded the 1945 Pan-African Congress to become a symbol of African independence.[20]

It did not take long for the revolutionary-minded Nkrumah to fall out with the leadership of the UGCC. Just eighteen months after his return to the Gold Coast, he split from the organization and formed the Convention People's Party (CPP), whose motto was "Self-government now." Nkrumah forged the CPP into a modern political machine with a newspaper, flags, youth groups, and a political platform. In fiery speeches to people across the country—homeless boys sleeping on the verandas of the wealthy, trade unionists, ex-servicemen, bureaucrats, traders, school-

First president of Ghana, Kwame Nkrumah, at a political rally in 1957. Screenshot from *African Independence*.

teachers, market women, the frustrated and impatient—Nkrumah called for them to "Seek ye first the political kingdom and all things shall be added unto it." As Gandhi had done in India, Nkrumah promoted a campaign of "positive action," which involved mass protest against the colonial government through strikes, boycotts, and other forms of civil disobedience.[21] The CPP called for universal suffrage, including the vote for women and the elimination of any property requirements.

In my interview with Charles Menson, he directed my attention to the specific processes leading up to Ghanaian independence: "Civilians—they boycotted everything that the Europeans had brought. . . . And it is from there that a commission was set up to investigate all these disturbances."

K. B. Asante elaborated on these processes in Ghana:

There was a split as to how fast they should move toward self-government. And Nkrumah broke away and formed the Gold Coast Convention. Because Nkrumah wanted self-government now, while the others were prepared for self-government to come as soon as possible or the foreseeable future. And therefore there were commissions to find out what should happen; we had elections, where Nkrumah proposed self-government now, and he won.

Before I left for England, I just wanted to be another high function-
ary in the colonial sector. Yes, that was what we believed. So Kwame
Nkrumah's revolution was to change how we talk about the African
personality, self-fulfillment, and self-confidence of the African. The
black man should know that he is as good as anybody else, and so on.
That was a major revolution. In actual practice, of course, you got to
give form to it, in self-government, in the way you do things, in trying
to get education widespread, in developing the economy, and so on.
But central to that was that revolution of changing of mind-set.

Rioting rocked the streets of Accra. Police dragged protestors away.
Governor Arden-Clarke declared a state of emergency and ordered the arrest of Nkrumah and the leadership of the CPP. The police booked and
handcuffed Nkrumah. He was convicted on three charges of incitement
and sedition by a criminal court and sentenced to three years' imprisonment, of which he served a year's time. He was undaunted. Foreshadowing
the future activities of Nelson Mandela, Nkrumah, in prison, continued
his efforts to draft a new constitution and led the movement to form and
elect a new Legislative Council with Africans as the majority. By the time
of his release, the CPP had become the most powerful political force in
the nation. The arrest and subsequent prison sentences of Nkrumah and his
colleagues turned them into heroes. Following a wave of enthusiasm, the
CPP exceeded the expectations of its own leadership and the world. The
CPP won thirty-four of the thirty-eight popularly contested seats, while
Danquah's UGCC won three.[22]

President Nkrumah's personal assistant, K. B. Asante, explained to me
how the idea of African equality became the basis for the fight for independence:

You see, years of slavery, years, and which was then followed by colonialism, had a great impact on the African. You see, there you had, even
during the slave trade, you had a people who believed in the sanctity
of the human person and so on. So why was it that Africans were being, or black people, were being treated differently? So they had to find
a reason to disparage the African character that he was not yet there.
Anyway, slavery was abolished, but the idea still stayed/remained. Then
came colonialism. And then, why should another people rule another?
You have to find reasons, and therefore, and then they were not, they
were not fit to rule themselves, and all that.

A positive change [Nkrumah] made was that he made Ghanaians believe to some extent in themselves. [Nkrumah] made Africans to realize

that they belong together—Africans not only on the continent, but in the diaspora—that they belong together.

Asante gave me some background on the events of 1948,

Things were changing in that we had many people who have had ex-posure outside, especially the soldiers, return to the Gold Coast. They had sort of been insulated. Now they went out to East Africa, to India, and Burma, and they came back and they had rubbed shoulders with the British. And they came back with the idea that, oh, these people are just like us, and why should we be in a subordinate position? And they had begun questioning their condition of life; they just couldn't take life as it was before. So they also wanted their rights. They wanted conditions of service to be better. So they marched to the castle, which was the seat of government, to present a petition to the governor. And they were prevented, not only prevented, but the British policeman in charge, Captain Imray, ordered the soldiers to fire. And three of them were killed, and of course they therefore rushed through town, destroy-ing and burning things, and they were helped by the people. So there was a temporary breakdown of law and order. And that was the route which preceded independence.

In 1951, Kwame Nkrumah, the joint secretary of the Fifth Pan-African Congress, squatted on a prison floor eating a bowl of maize porridge with-out sugar in his crowded cell at James Fort Prison in Accra, Gold Coast. He must have pondered how the road from the dreams and resolutions of the gathering in Manchester led to a prison cell. He must have wondered what lay before him on the other side of the prison gates, or maybe he thought about the significance of his recent election victory. He had recently been elected to the Legislative Assembly for Accra Central and was waiting to be told when he would be released.

The newsreels of Nkrumah's release show exuberant crowds greeting him as he leaves the prison. The mixed expressions of pride, joy, and en-thusiasm for a new day appear to be celebrated by the people. As Nkrumah parts the crowds in his newfound leadership, we are given a visual sense of the changing political direction.

Across town from James Fort Prison, behind the high white walls of Christiansborg Castle, a seventeenth-century fort built for slaving and home to British governors for the past fifty years, Sir Charles Arden-Clarke was forced to sign the release orders for the prisoner, an act that would forever change British colonial rule in Africa. In his view, Nkrumah was a danger-ous man who represented the "communist" threat.[23] Yet Arden-Clarke invited him to visit Christiansborg Castle. The governor and ex-convict met and discussed the next steps toward "self-government." Nkrumah left the governor's castle with instructions to form a government. He had made the transition from convict to leader of government business. In 1952, Nkrumah's title was changed to prime minister.[24] He would later recount, "As I walked down the steps, it was as if the whole thing had been a dream, that I was stepping down from the clouds and that I would soon wake up and find myself squatting on the prison floor eating a bowl of maize porridge."[25]

By that time, the British and French governors in Africa had come to terms with nationalist politicians whom they had previously labeled as extremist agitators. But Nkrumah was different. He described himself as "a non-denominational Christian and a Marxist Socialist." In his meeting with the governor, he was "unalterably opposed to imperialism in any form," and he made it clear that he would settle for nothing less than full independence. A shockwave hit Africa, causing alarm and inspiration at the same time.[26]

After winning the 1954 election, Nkrumah's CPP made progress toward independence. During an earlier visit to the United States, where he gave a commencement address at his alma mater, Lincoln University,

Kwame Nkrumah and others on the evening of Ghanaian independence, 1957. Screenshot from *African Independence*.

he explained, "What we want is the right to govern ourselves, or even to misgovern ourselves."[27] The victory in 1954 was another step closer to this objective. In 1956, the CPP won 72 of 104 seats. The Gold Coast would be granted its independence on March 6, 1957.[28]

After years of political organizing and prison, Nkrumah knew that the Gold Coast's time had finally come. On March 6, 1957, Nkrumah proudly stood before a crowd of tens of thousands as the Union Jack flag was lowered and the new Ghanaian national flag of red, gold, and green was raised. With tears streaming down his face, Nkrumah declared Ghana's sovereignty and independence. A new era of the independence movement in Africa was born.[29]

I spoke to Nkrumah's daughter Samia Nkrumah, a member of the Ghanaian parliament, at the Nkrumah Memorial Park in Accra, Ghana. I asked her why everybody marks 1957 in Ghana as the beginning of the movement for independence on the African continent. She responded,

> Okay, to start with, Ghana was the first Sub-Saharan African country to gain independence. But what is significant is the moment Ghana won independence, it started helping other liberation movements, actively helping them. And there are many, many stories to be told, from helping Algeria, the liberation movements in Algeria, to Guinea, to Southern Africa—everywhere. And that is why three years later, 1960, which is the year we call the Africa Year, the Year of Africa, seventeen countries gained independence. It was not a coincidence. It was not a coincidence. Ghana was actively helping liberation movements in various ways. In fact, in '58, there was an All-African People's Conference here in Accra where many would-be leaders of African states were present, attended. So there was a vision to help other countries become politically independent. And that confirms Kwame Nkrumah's statement on the eve of independence.
>
> Ghana, through Kwame Nkrumah, had put forward a list of proposals to help us unite as a continent—common currency, common markets, common citizenship, and borderless continents, central bank, common foreign policy, and different strategy. In short, a list of proposals and projects that Europe went to implement years after. So we know that we are pioneers in unity.

New leaders with democratic dreams for their new nations gave Africa and the world hope. At such a time in history, many things seemed possible. And nothing captured this more than the movement in Ghana—the beacon of African independence. I asked His Excellency John Kufuor to place Nkrumah's relevance in historical context:

Interview with Her Excellency Samia Nkrumah, member of Parliament (2009–2012), daughter of President Kwame Nkrumah, in Accra, Ghana, 2011. Jabari Zuberi/TZ Production Company.

Very relevant. It's not as yet even fully realized or fulfilled. Nkrumah was perhaps talking more politics than economics then. Now the world talks markets. The bigger your markets, the more attractive you are. I believe this is the power of China, and India, and this European Union. Everybody has seen the sense of combining to create a sizable market in the globalization process. So Nkrumah's statement, that statement, I believe was quite prophetic. Whether he appreciated the economics of it or not, it was prophetic, and his place in history I believe is above question. He led in the Pan-African struggle . . . saw Africa as one continent of the same people who should come together to command the respect of the rest of the world. Very good.

This same struggle would repeat itself over and over, everywhere on the African continent.[30]

THE SPREAD OF THE MOVEMENT

Nkrumah's dream was that Ghana's independence would spark a movement leading to the independence of the entire continent and that this

Interview with John Kufuor, president of Ghana (2001–2009), in Accra, Ghana, 2011. Screenshot from *African Independence*.

independence would result in a United States of Africa. While Ghana's achievement of independence mirrored the efforts of freedom movements elsewhere in Africa, there was a key difference. For Nkrumah, it wasn't enough that Ghana became independent. Before an immense crowd of his countrymen on the day of their independence, he announced, "At last, Ghana, your beloved country, is free forever!" As he continued, Nkrumah declared to his newly liberated audience that freedom was an inalienable right of *all* Africans, not just a few: "We again rededicate ourselves in the struggle to emancipate other countries in Africa, for our independence is meaningless unless it is linked up with the total liberation of the African continent." More so than in the Sudan, Morocco, and Tunisia, Ghana tied its future to the rest of Africa, whereas, at times, leaders of the other three newly independent nations saw their future more closely tied to the Middle East. Nkrumah was determined to make Ghana's capital, Accra, the center of African independence and liberation. Accra would serve as a base from which nationalist leaders could work for independence and Pan-Africanism more generally.[31]

The idea of a Sixth Pan-African Congress was reconfigured when delegates from all over the continent met in December 1958 in Accra. The All-African People's Congress brought together over two hundred still-unknown political leaders of the African independence movement as well as known figures such as Nkrumah and Kenneth Kaunda. Many of these politicians, union leaders, women, and youth organization leaders gained prominence in the years ahead. Pan-Africanism moved from the realm of ideas espoused by Du Bois and his fellow intellectual activists into the practical politics of building African independence.[32]

By 1957, in the French colonial territories, the Rassemblement Democratique Africain held its third congress in Bamako, the capital of French Sudan (Mali after 1960). At this congress, the dissidents were given a new forum. The meeting was adjourned over the issue of African autonomy from France. Political rivalry among African leaders would weaken the RDA, and at the decisive historical moment of independence, West and Equatorial Africa would act as divergent political units.

The French government was near collapse as a consequence of its inability to deal with the armed uprisings in its former colonies. Under the threat of a military coup and a call for General de Gaulle's return to power, the Fifth Republic was created under his leadership. General de Gaulle's solution for the colonies played upon the political differences among the African leaders, as is evident in his referendum for French West and Equatorial Africa. His proposal gave each colony three choices: *immediate independence* with the cession of French aid and the withdrawal of all French personnel, become a *French overseas department*, or have *internal self-government* while France oversaw foreign policy, economics, currency, and defense.

Under General de Gaulle's leadership, France proposed a Franco-African Community to all of its colonial possessions. The French policy of decolonization sought to bring its West African colonies into a close union with France. It seems to have been a matter of national pride for the French government that the colonies would choose to remain "French." The British decolonization process led them to develop the "Commonwealth," which included the former colonial areas. The French replaced the ideas of "colonies" and "empire" with the notion of "Francophonie."

At a time when French West Africa consisted of the area now known as Mauritania, Mali, Senegal, Guinea, the Ivory Coast, Burkina Faso, Benin, and Niger, a future freedom fighter, Sékou Touré, was born. At that time, the entire area formed one administrative unit administered from Dakar under the colonial French. The independence movement was changing Africa, and Africa's relationship with the West could not be taken for granted.

The "no" vote by the people of Guinea in the 1958 de Gaulle referendum on becoming part of the French Community was historic. Only Guinea opted for immediate independence! Touré would say, "There is no dignity without freedom. . . . We prefer freedom in poverty to riches in slavery."[33] On October 2, 1958, Guinea gained its independence from

France. The infuriated French severed all economic ties with Guinea and withdrew its civil servants, doctors, teachers, and so forth immediately. It was not long before the other French colonies, gradually and with a less confrontational manner, followed suit.

The French constitution was modified in 1960 to allow members of the French colonial community to become independent. The conservatives had out-maneuvered the radical wing of the RDA, and West and Equatorial Africa were split into twelve states. Between October 1960 and March 1961, the French colonies in Sub-Saharan Africa held three conferences to discuss and decide the nature of their newly won freedom.

In October 1960, they met in the capital of the Ivory Coast, Abidjan, and discussed the Belgian Congo, Algeria, and Mauritania. Morocco was claiming Mauritania as part of its territory and refused to recognize its independence; however, the United Nations had approved its independence. The nations in attendance at the meeting agreed to adopt a common foreign policy and became known as the Abidjan Group.

The second meeting took place in the winter of 1960 in Brazzaville in the Congo (formerly the French Congo). The conference was also preoccupied with the Belgian Congo crisis. The attendees distinguished themselves by adopting a conservative pro-French position. The twelve nations in attendance were thereafter known as the Brazzaville Group and included Cameroon, the Central African Republic, Chad, the Congo (Brazzaville), Dahomey, Gabon, the Ivory Coast, Malagasy, Mauritania, Niger, Senegal, and the Upper Volta. Guinea and Mali were not part of this conference or the Brazzaville Group even though they were part of the former French West Africa. The Brazzaville Group took the position of cooperation in economic, political, and cultural affairs and of "non-interference in the affairs of other countries."

In March 1961, the Brazzaville Group met in Yaoundé, Cameroon. They set up the Organization Africaine et Malagache de Coopération Economique (OAMCE; Afro-Malagasy Organization for Economic Cooperation). They also set up an airline for member countries called Air Afrique.[34]

New political leadership led movements to challenge the dependent status of the African continent. A number of defining conferences followed the 1958 Accra meeting. Rival groups in the movement emerged. Various factions reflected different strategies toward independence. The Monrovia Group advocated a more conservative and conciliatory path, while the more radical Casablanca Group called for immediate independence and collaboration with the West and Soviet blocs.[35]

Professional and cultural leaders also joined the debate by holding several Pan-African gatherings. "Negro writers and artists" from all over Africa and the diaspora met at two conferences, one in Paris in 1956 and the other in Rome in 1959. The African Conference on the Rule of Law convened in Lagos in 1961. Close to two hundred lawyers and jurists met in the Nigerian city and proclaimed their commitment to human rights and the rule of law on the African continent.[36]

By 1960, the African call for independence was clear. Even France and Britain came to recognize that the old game of colonialism was over. In February 1960, the prime minster of Great Britain, Harold Macmillan, came to South Africa to speak to the parliament in Cape Town. He had received a lot of criticism for his planned visit to South Africa as people thought it was wrong for him to visit the country because of its apartheid government. The government had implemented a system of legal racial segregation. Africans and other racially marginalized groups were prevented from fully participating in the political, economic, and social life of the nation. In 1960, a visit to the apartheid government by a political leader was considered by many to be a bad thing to do, especially for a high-ranking member of the British government. But Macmillan was on his way, and his critics had to take a seat when they heard the content of his speech. This is what he had to say:

> Fifteen years ago this movement spread through Asia. Many countries there, of different races and civilizations, pressed their claim to an independent national life. Today, the same thing is happening in Africa.[37]

Macmillan correctly dated the movement back fifteen years, placing it at the end of World War II in 1945. The wind of change, as he put it, blew all over Asia as people stood up and claimed their national citizenship and demanded an end to colonialism and independence. The African independence movement had been born, and it was spreading all over Africa, so that by 1960 it was undeniable that independence was coming to the African continent. He continued:

> The most striking of all the impressions I have formed since I left London a month ago is of the strength of this African national consciousness. In different places it takes different forms, but it is happening everywhere. The wind of change is blowing through this continent, and, whether we like it or not, this growth of national consciousness is a political fact. We must all accept it as a fact.[38]

Harold MacMillan, prime minister of Britain (1957–1963), at a meeting on African independence in London, 1960. Screenshot from *African Independence.*

At his home in Dar es Salaam, His Excellency Ali Hassan Mwinyi described to me the impact of Macmillan's speech on the movement:

> That was long after, very long after we had started. That was not a new thing at all. It was pronouncing ideas that we had already. And we felt very, very happy indeed because we thought it was only the South Africans, the Boers, who needed that speech. The rest of us were ready for it. In fact, we were working towards achieving what he was telling the Boers in South Africa.

His Excellency Rupiah Banda, president of Zambia from 2008 to 2011, had this to say about the "Winds of Change" speech:

> I'm almost certain that it had the same impact on me as it had on you and on most of us, black people all over Africa, all Africans. Because don't forget that Mr. Macmillan was the prime minster from the conservative party of the United Kingdom, and one would have expected him to support colonialism, continued colonialism, but it was significant that he said what he said. And the impact was so overwhelming right across Africa. I remember very clear. I was a young man then. And it was such

**His Excellency Ali Hassan
Mwinyi, president of
Tanzania (1985–1995), Dar
es Salaam, Tanzania, 2010.
Jabari Zuberi/TZ Production
Company.**

a wonderful . . . to hear that even they think it's possible. So why should
I be doubting myself? And so we intensified our fight for liberation.

African national flags would be newly minted in the decades following
Nkrumah's declaration at the Ghana independence celebrations: Nigeria,
Sierra Leone, Tanzania, Uganda, Kenya, Malawi, Zambia, Gambia, Botswana, Lesotho, Mauritius, Benin, Cameroon, the Central African Republic, Chad, Gabon, the Ivory Coast, Madagascar, Mali, Mauritania, Niger,
Senegal, Togo, the Upper Volta, Algeria, and Burundi. All had gained
their independence within a decade of Nkrumah declaring Ghana's independence. And all accomplished independence as a result of non-violent
political action.

Not everyone agreed with the direction of the winds of independence. I visited the last South African president of the apartheid regime,
F. W. de Klerk, at his office in Cape Town. Macmillan's speech had argued
that the world and Africa were changing and that these changes required
colonial governments and South Africa's apartheid government to change

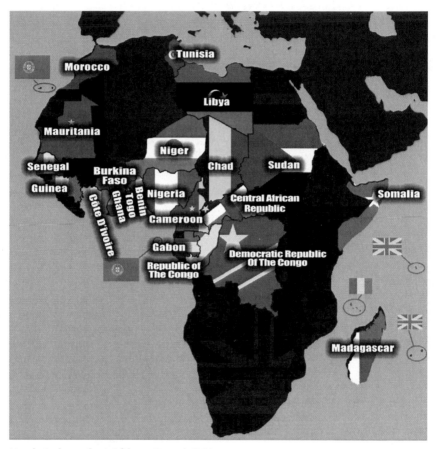

Newly Independent African States, 1960

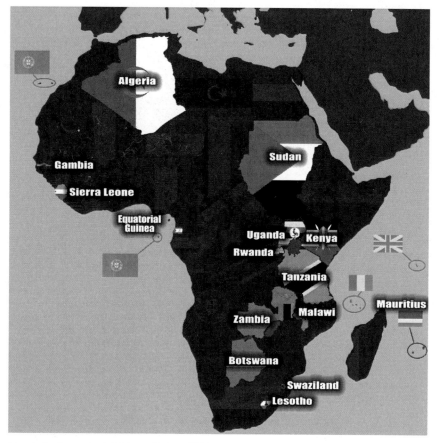

Newly Independent African States, 1970

their national politics. Given this, I asked de Klerk how the "Winds of Change" speech affected his politics:

> It made everybody of course think, because it was a far-reaching speech, but generally speaking the party as it then was—I was just out of university; I wasn't part of it—in the end reacted negatively, because it showed according to their interpretation a lack of understanding for my people, the Afrikaner people. This tendency to deal with the Afrikaner at that stage in the same breath as you were dealing with colonialism was rejected by the party, because the Afrikaners fought the first modern anti-colonial freedom war on the soil of South Africa against Great Britain. In 1834, there was a Great Trek. People weren't happy with British rule here in the Cape Province and moved into the hinterland of South Africa. Established finally two republics. Republics, full democratic republics, governed themselves from the 1840, 1850s, right until the end of that century, and then gold and diamonds were discovered. And then suddenly the British started to get very interested, and in the end, the Anglo-Boer War took place. It took them three years to subjugate the Afrikaner of those two republics. It is against that background, that there was a feeling that the concept of self-determination for the Afrikaner people should be given space in international thinking. And it was on that foundation of saying we governed ourselves in the past, we have good relations with other black African nations in South Africa who governed themselves, the Zulus, the Xhosas, the Sothos, the Tswanas. And we want a country and a land in which we govern ourselves. That

The Voortrekker Monument commemorating the Great Trek (1835–1854), in Pretoria, South Africa, 2008. Screenshot from *African Independence*.

Interview with President F. W. de Klerk, last head of state during the apartheid era (1989–1994) at his office in Cape Town, South Africa, 2008. Screenshot from *African Independence*.

was the moral justification for apartheid, which then became a separate development. It was the same concept that the whole world now supports for Israel and Palestine, divide the land on the basis of ethnicity . . . on the basis of having nation-states for each identifiable nation, but it failed in South Africa.

The end of World War II meant decolonization for most of Africa. The destruction of European economies and US opposition to colonial monopolies meant that classical colonialism was on its deathbed. However, in South Africa, apartheid was born in 1948.[39] This form of racial segregation was enshrined in laws enacted by the National Party governments that ruled South Africa between 1948 and 1994. Avenues for peaceful social protest in South Africa and elsewhere on the African continent were being violently curtailed.

POWER OF THE GUN

Like Ghana, other African nations, including Tanzania and Zambia, provided critical assistance in the Pan-African struggle for independence. Many of the newly independent nations did not attain their independence using the gun. Yet they would support the use of the gun in other freedom struggles. Zambia had gained its independence through political agitation and through organizing various political parties into one party. It was felt that the multitude of parties could more effectively fight against colonial rule if they were unified. His Excellency Kenneth Kaunda explained this process to me:

> We had a duty to assist our colleagues in Angola, west of us; Mozambique, east of us under the Portuguese. Zimbabwe, Southern Rhodesia in those days, because we were Northern Rhodesia—they were under the British settlers. South Africa, Boers and the British mixed to form apartheid. In Namibia, same thing. Namibia had to be under the Germans before that.
>
> Mahatma Gandhi's student, Pandit Nehru, the first prime minister of India, wrote like this, in one of his books—When you are fighting against British colonialism, you can afford to fight in a non-violent way. "Non-violent way" meant defying unjust laws, being sent to prison for that. Coming out continually until you won. We followed that path.
>
> But when you are fighting other colonial powers, you can't afford to do that. You've got to fight using the gun. So I could see that. He was very right.

Kaunda's comments underscore the fact that the independence movement was international. African leaders learned from the movements in Asia and other parts of the world. They also received support from these newly independent nations in their fight for political independence, justice, and equality.

For example, Sukarno led Indonesia's nationalist movement to declare independence from the Netherlands in 1945; this unilateral declaration of independence came six months after the defeat of Germany. Indonesia was formally granted independence in 1949. The British lost one of their principal colonies with the independence of India. The legendary non-violent leadership of Mahatma Gandhi proved to be decisive, and the British parliament passed the Indian Independence Act of 1947. No sooner had this happened than Pakistan declared its nationhood.[40]

Another important example occurred immediately following the end of the war. The French reoccupied Indochina (Vietnam) because the area had been lost to the Japanese during the war. Opposed to these efforts, Ho Chi Minh, the Vietnamese nationalist leader and attendee of the 1945 Pan-African Congress, declared independence from France. A guerilla war against colonialism followed. After eight years of fighting and being utterly dependent on US financial backing to fight the war, France requested a cease-fire in May 1954. The world was not surprised. During those years, the Cold War accelerated, and Vietnam became one of the spaces in which the war was fought. In North Vietnam, you had Soviet and Chinese support directed at the socialists, and in South Vietnam, Western support was to be found.

These events did not go without notice in Africa. Kaunda continued to expound on the lesson learned about supporting other African nations in the movement for independence:

> For our colleagues in the other countries around us, we had to help fight in a violent way using the gun, using weapons. How would we help them? I determined for our independence we had to allow our colleagues to pass through Northern Rhodesia, to come to Tanzania, here under Mwalimu Julius Nyerere, who found places for them in the country where they would go and train how to go and fight for their independence.

By this time, the Algerian nationalists had formed the Front de Libération Nationale (the FLN), which represented the aspirations of a younger generation of Algerian nationalists. This generation did not call for self-government or home rule but demanded the independence of Algeria from France. The French government continued to support the European settlers, and war followed.

By 1954, Algeria's European settler population numbered almost a million; the "native" Berber and Arab numbers had risen to around nine million. The Africans were crowded into the less productive part of the land, without capital to develop it and with no funds for social services. As a result, living standards were low, unemployment was high in the rural areas and the cities, and 90 percent of the population was illiterate. There were less than two hundred Algerian doctors and pharmacists.

Unlike Morocco, Algeria had no royal family to rally nationalist opinion. And unlike Tunisia, they had no established political party or trade union movement to consolidate plans of action. However, they did have men with military experience in the French army. These veterans had some Western education and developed nationalistic perspectives and revolutionary orientations that were suited to the Algerian realities. They were aware of the changes occurring in the world. They knew of the French defeats in the war and in Indochina. They knew about the independence movements in Egypt, Libya, Tunisia, and other parts of Africa and Asia. For these new elite, independence seemed like a possibility. Later they also attracted members of the educated elite and important leaders of Islamic thought. Independence was in the air.

The French, however, were not so ready to give up Algeria. They had much to lose. In addition to the political influence of nearly a million *pieds-noirs*—the white settlers—France had substantial investments in agriculture and mining. And the recent discovery of oil and natural gas in the Sahara offered considerable oil wealth on its "own territory." This may be why the socialist minister of the interior François Mitterrand proclaimed to the National Assembly, "Algeria is France. And who among you . . . would hesitate to employ every means to preserve France?" When Mollet went to Algiers in February 1956 to discuss the possibility of transition, the settlers pelted him with rotten food. The day would become known as the "Day of the Tomatoes." Settlers established the pro-colony Committee for the Defense of French Algeria. Not long after, the first shots were fired. The war accelerated.[41]

The Algerian movement for independence was one of the most pro-longed and violent examples of decolonization. The French were engaged in a bitter war of attrition with the FLN. Two FLN leaders, Ahmed Zabana and Abdel-kader Ferradj, were arrested and sentenced to death for murder to satiate the Algerian settlers' demand for retribution against the actions of the FLN's military wing. Zabana and Ferradj were guillotined in June 1956. Their executions led the FLN to accelerate the armed conflict into the "Battle of Algiers" that same year.[42]

In December 1956, following a series of FLN assassinations and European reprisals, the Mollet government authorized Colonel Jacques Massu to use extreme measures to destroy, once and for all, the FLN. In 1957, it appeared that Colonel Massu had succeeded. He had broken a general strike and crushed the FLN in the Battle of Algiers. The next year the French air force bombed Sakhiet, a town across the border in Tunisia, which purportedly was a base for the FLN. Yet the European settlers feared that Paris would abandon their cause. On April 25, thousands of settlers rallied in Algeria and demanded continued French support and the return of de Gaulle to power. This and other forms of protest inside both France and Algeria made de Gaulle's return a serious possibility.

De Gaulle took office on June 1, 1958. A few days later, on June 4, he flew to Algiers. There, from the balcony of the governor general's palace, he announced, "I have understood you," to enthusiastic soldiers and settlers.[43] The prime minister was very popular in France, where he received 80 percent of the vote in the September 1958 referendum; in Algeria, he secured an astounding 96 percent. Once in office he established the authority of government in France and sought to quickly resolve the war in Algeria. The political winds had shifted against colonialism, and international support was increasingly turning toward the FLN. It would take de Gaulle one year to propose "self-determination" for Algeria. During the Algerian war, about two million French soldiers served; 60 percent of them were conscripts. The settlers and French military were not happy, and they protested, plotted, and spoke of revolution. But all efforts to reverse de Gaulle's position failed, even an unsuccessful military putsch. By June 1960, de Gaulle was in talks with the FLN. After two years of negotiations, Algeria declared its independence on July 3, 1962. French rule in northern Africa was over.[44]

Newsreels of the time show the intensity of the protest and the strong support among the Algerian people for independence. The Algerian War for Independence led to one of the most important incendiary epics in filmmaking with Gillo Pontecorvo's 1966 *The Battle of Algiers*. Analysts have noted the influence of Frantz Fanon's 1961 book *The Wretched of the Earth* as a Pan-African intellectual source from which *The Battle of Algiers* draws, despite Pontecorvo's denying "any direct citation from Fanon" in a 2003 interview. Fanon saw violence as an essential component to colonial rule and thought the only way for it to be removed was by violence.[45] This radical perspective was embodied by the lives of Algerian men, women, and children. We have yet to witness anything better than this quasi-documentary film, which memorably portrays the war of attrition between the French army and the FLN guerillas.

Settlers in East Africa also proved to be a formidable force. While the Africans were consolidating the movement for independence, the settlers in Kenya wanted the same treatment as their brethren in South Africa and Southern Rhodesia. The settlers in South Africa had formed in 1910 the Union of South Africa, which brought together the four separate British colonies of Cape Colony, Natal Colony, Transvaal Colony, and Orange Colony and established a constitutional monarchy similar to the Canadian system. Likewise, in 1923, the white settlers in Southern Rhodesia won internal self-government. At the same time, the number of white colonial settlers on the African continent increased, so much so that the white settler populations in Southern Rhodesia and Kenya doubled after World War II. The European Highlands of Kenya were opened to British veterans, and at the same time the Kikuyu were forced onto "native reserves."

The white settlers promoted a federation of three East African colonies—Kenya, Uganda, and Tanganyika—under a white minority regime. Settlers campaigned to secure their own privileged positions. They spoke with envious tones of the achievements of the National Party in South Africa, and within the colonial context, they wanted white minority rule in the whole of British East Africa. The wartime demand for Kenyan agricultural goods had caused an economic boom that transformed the settlement into a profitable venture, and post-war London looked to the colony to help it through its reconstruction.

Freedom fighters such as Dedan Kimathi used guerilla warfare against the British. Kimathi was one of the leaders of the Mau Mau freedom fighters. The Mau Mau brought British colonialism in East Africa to its knees and shook the very foundation of its meaning. A primary school teacher, Kimathi hailed from a small village in Kenya. In 1940 he enlisted in the British army to join the fight against fascism. After one month, he was discharged from the British army. In the mid-1940s he began working with the Kenya African Union, becoming the organization's secretary for the branch at Ol Kalou that was under the influence of the Mau Mau freedom fighters. In the early 1950s, Kimathi took the oath of the Mau Mau, and along with the likes of Jomo Kenyatta and Waruhiu Itote (also known as General China), Kimathi became a leader of the independence movement.

Jomo Kenyatta had attended the 1945 Pan-African Congress with Nkrumah and Du Bois, and he returned to Kenya from working and studying in London in 1946 to become a leader of the independence movement. He collaborated with the other leaders in the fight and was arrested for

Statue of Dedan Kimathi, Kenyan freedom fighter, in Nairobi, Kenya, 2008. Screenshot from *African Independence*.

Statue of Mzee Jomo Kenyatta, the first president of Kenya between 1964 and 1978, in Nairobi, Kenya, 2008. Screenshot from *African Independence*.

his leadership activities. General China was a veteran of the Kings African Rifles, and during World War II he served the British army in Ceylon and in Burma, attaining the rank of corporal. He returned from the war, became politically active, and ultimately got involved with the Kenya African National Union. Taken together, the three figures represented the coming together of the various strands of freedom fighters for the independence movement. However, because of Itote's agreement to cooperate with the government after his arrest, only Kenyatta and Kimathi are heralded as two of the most important leaders of the independence movement in Kenya.[46]

I visited Eloise Mukami Kimathi, freedom fighter from the Land and Freedom Army and Dedan Kimathi's widow, for an inside view about the relationship between him and Kenyatta.[47]

> Kenyatta and Kimathi used to meet often, and they all had a common objective of getting our freedom back. It was passed that even if all people were killed and only a boy and a girl were left, the community would still continue. We all agreed we were ready to be killed in order for the African to gain independence.

Mrs. Kimathi explained that Dedan Kimathi taught that Africans were equal to whites and that they had the same color of blood and worshipped the same god.

The Mau Mau emerged from Kenya's mass peasant movement. In Kenya, the Kikuyu were dramatically affected by settler colonialism. They were an agriculturalist people, and thus their way of life was devastated by the colonial government policy of land expropriation for European settlement. The Kikuyu had lost tens of thousands of acres that became the most productive European farmland in the colony. The hypocrisy of the civilizing mission of colonialism, made clear by African participation in the liberation of Europeans during World War II, was evident in Kenya. In response to the settler demand for special treatment, African discontent with the inequities of British colonial rule galvanized the ardent nationalism of the Kikuyu-based movement. Given the struggle over land, the movement for Kenyan independence was clearly connected to the importance of recapturing the land for Africans. Between 1952 and 1960, the British government killed and tortured hundreds of thousands of Kikuyu freedom fighters.[48]

For Africans, the colonial government established residential reserves in officially defined rural areas. These reserves were modeled on the homelands in South Africa and the reservations in the United States. For example, the Kikuyu had a set of reserves in the Central Province; the Luo were expected to live in the Nyanza Province Reserves. These reserves were too small for the population, and the land was ill suited for agricultural activities. Consequently, Africans were forced to work on European farms, the very farms that had been taken from them in the name of colonial development. Men leaving their reserve had to carry a pass called a *kipande*, which became one of the most hated symbols of British colonialism. Failure to produce this card on demand brought a fine and/or imprisonment.

Mrs. Kimathi, one of the many female leaders among the freedom fighters, reminds us of the importance of land in the struggle for independence:

> There's no freedom without land, and there's no land without freedom. Where there's land, there's wealth. That is where a person is able to help his or her child. Without a purpose and without land, he can't help his own children.

In my conversation with Mrs. Kimathi, she explained her life as a freedom fighter and the dream of independence in Kenya. She outlined how she and her colleagues came to the conclusion that arms were necessary in order to achieve this goal.

Kimathi and Kenyatta fought for independence, which eventually led to both of them being detained by the colonial powers. I asked Mrs.

Kimathi about the circumstances surrounding the capture of her late husband.[49]

> I was in detention that time. I was detained because I was Kimathi's
> wife, and I refused to show them where Kimathi was. So the colonial
> government treated me inhumanly, because I would not betray my husband by revealing to them where he was hiding. He was not arrested by
> hand. He was shot. He was not able to run after he was shot.
>
> They put some handcuffs on him at the point when he was shot.
> They put him in a car. He was taken to Nyeri Hospital so that the bullet
> wound would be treated. Then after he had been treated, he recovered.
>
> He was hanged because he said that Africans should rule themselves,
> and the land was the Africans'. He was asked to surrender, but he would
> never surrender.

It cost Kimathi his life. It cost Jomo Kenyatta nine years in prison.
But the Mau Mau freedom fighters go down as one of the pillars of East
Africa's independence movement. As Kimathi would say, "It is better to
die on our feet than to live on our knees." Ultimately Kenya gained its
independence in 1963.

British efforts to maintain the colonial status quo for its white brethren
failed politically. The London colonial office was forced to admit that mistakes had been committed and that the policy of torture was wrong. The
fight against the Mau Mau had cost the Crown fifty-five million pounds.
Pacifying the natives had become too costly. The war convinced Britain
that political independence along with continued economic dependence
was the most viable way to maintain in Africa what was left of British
influence.[50]

A similar, and maybe even more violent, struggle for independence
took place in the areas colonized by Portugal. Reminiscent of Macmillan's
1960 recommendations to the South African parliament, General Antonio
Spinola's 1974 book, *Portugal and the Future*, repeated what was common
political knowledge in Portugal at the time. The Portuguese government
commissioned his report in 1970, when Spinola was still the governor general of Guinea-Bissau. In both the report and the book, Spinola suggested
the need to change the colonial relationship into a "Lusophone" community. In this new political arrangement, more power would be given to the
colonies. General Spinola's report was read as an admission that the colonial
wars were unwinnable.

After the publication of his book, the general was fired. However, a
few months later the army seized power in Lisbon and installed Spinola as

**Samora Machel, first president of Mozambique, receiving Mozambique's indepen-
dence in Lusaka, Zambia, in 1975. Screenshot from *African Independence*.**

head of the military Junta of National Salvation. The junta suppressed Spinola's recommendation of a Lusophone community with their own policy
in support of decolonization. By July, the junta's political base passed a law
in which the Portuguese government accepted the right of self-determination, up to and including independence. Following the passage of this
law, Portuguese officials negotiated a peaceful military withdrawal. Soon
afterward, they recognized the independence movement in Guinea-Bissau
and Cape Verde, followed by Mozambique, Angola, and the island group
of São Tomé and Príncipe.[51]

African freedom fighters in colonies with a large European population
had to fight bloody wars to end racial domination. However, for members
of the independence movement, white resistance to African freedom was
not read in racial terms. I sat down with His Excellency Pedro Pires of the
republic of Cape Verde, who fought for the independence of Cape Verde
and Guinea-Bissau alongside Amílcar Cabral, to understand the significance
of this dimension of the fight.[52]

I don't know, but the issue is in the following. It is in the attitude of the
population of European origin, in the attitude—if they are in favor of

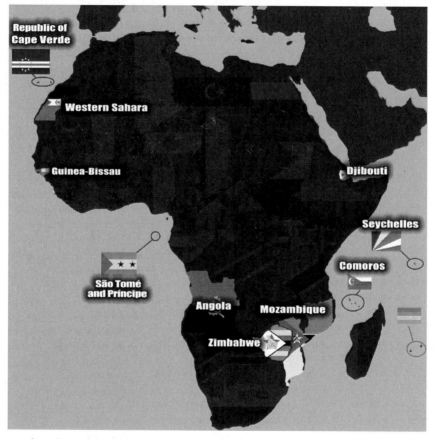

Newly Independent African States, 1980

the liberation of the majority, or if they are against it. If they are against the liberation of the majority, they are on the side of the colonizer. If they are in favor of the liberation of the majority, they will be on the side of the colonized, of the one who is seeking his or her freedom. Therefore, it is not a condemnation, but it is an attitude, a position. But there are other facts that should be taken into account. It is the settlement of those populations—under what conditions they established settlement and what privileges they had, what violence they committed against the African populations, black or others. Was this settlement a violent one, or was it peaceful? Therefore it all depends on the historical circumstances.

But the fight for national liberation is not directed against anyone for his or her color, but instead for his or her position, his or her attitude.

The great freedom fighter Nelson Mandela's words foreshowed President Pires's comments after his release from prison on February 11, 1990. During a visit to the White House, Mandela responded to President George H. W. Bush's criticism of armed struggle in the South African fight for political independence.

PRESIDENT BUSH. And from all parties we look for a clear and unequivocal commitment to negotiations leading to peaceful change. I call on all elements in South African society to renounce the use of violence in armed struggle, break free from this cycle of repression and violent reaction that breeds nothing but more fear and suffering.

Interview with Pedro Verona Rodrigues Pires, president of Cape Verde (2001–2011), Johannesburg, South Africa, 2012. Screenshot from *African Independence*.

NELSON MANDELA. I will also inform him about developments as far as the armed struggle is concerned. The remarks that he has made here are due to the fact that he has not as yet got a proper briefing from us. I might just state in passing that the methods of political action used by the black people of South Africa were determined by the South African government. As long as the government is prepared to talk, to maintain channels of communication between itself and the governed, there can be no question of violence whatsoever. But when a government decides to ban political organizations of the oppressed, intensifies oppression, and does not allow any free political activity no matter how peaceful and non-violent, then the people have no alternative but to resort to violence. There is not a single political organization in our country inside and outside parliament which can ever compare with the African National Congress in its total commitment to peace. If we are forced to resort to violence, it is because we have no other alternative whatsoever.

THE AFRICAN MILITARY IN THE COLD WAR

All corners of African society were bracing for their entrance into independence and a post-colonial world in the aftermath of World War II, and into

Nelson Mandela, shortly after being released from prison, and President George Bush at the White House in 1990. Screenshot from *African Independence*.

the frying pan of the new era of Cold War politics. Even African soldiers were finding new opportunities to advance their own status in these new circumstances. As one of the most educated and organized groups in post-colonial Africa, the higher-ranking African soldier has played a key role in post-independence Africa.

The Africanization of the military became increasingly important in the era of independence. French colonial authorities were the first to recognize the importance of Africanizing the officers of its colonial troops—the Tirailleurs Sénégalais. In the 1950s, they began to actively change their image and increase their efforts to attract new recruits from educated young Africans. The new French program, called "La Promotion Africaine," proved to be quite successful. In 1956, a special training school for African officers was revived as the Ecole de Formation des Officiers du Régime Transitore des Territores d'Outre Mer (EFORTOM). In 1958, under African pressure, because they resented the term "transitional regime," the name was changed to Ecole de Formation des Officiers Ressortisants des Territoires d'Outre-Mer (Training School for Those from Overseas Territories).

The EFORTOM school survived the independence movement and continued to graduate an average of twenty Africans a year. The newly independent former French colonies established a series of bilateral military agreements in the years immediately following independence until the school closed its doors in 1965.

EFORTOM was a primary source for the creation of the military elite in the French-speaking African nations. In 1956, the standing army consisted of thirty-four thousand soldiers and only sixty-eight African officers (seventeen second lieutenants and thirty-four lieutenants). These graduates would become civilian as well as military leaders. The graduates are a who's who of African military presidents and aspiring presidents in the post-colonial era. The list would include Seyni Kountché, class of 1959, who served as president of Niger from 1974 to 1987; Mathieu Kérékou, class of 1960, president of Benin from 1972 to 1991; Moussa Traoré, class of 1961, president of Mali from 1968 to 1991; and Saye Zerbo, president of the Upper Volta between 1980 and 1982 when he was overthrown. The soldiers all took power by force of arms and helped usher in the era of military dictatorship in Africa. Several of these men's fathers were soldiers, and as the sons of soldiers, they had been in the special military academies for the children of veterans. These soldiers played a unique role in the politics of African independence.

The British did not launch an Africanization plan for officers in the King's African Rifles in Kenya until 1957; and by 1961 they had produced only ten native officers. However, several important African leaders experienced some British military education. For example, in 1965, Muammar Abu Minyar al-Gaddafi (later known as Colonel Gaddafi) went to Britain for further training at the British Army Staff College (now the Joint Services Command and Staff College). While the British did not have as systematic a training system, the soldiers in British West Africa still played a decisive role in the independence of African republics.

The implications of the Africanization of the post-colonial armies were the rise of the soldier as a key element in the leadership of newly independent African states. Not understanding the post–World War II African soldier and losing control of the post-independence military became two of the major issues for the newly independent states, and this lack of understanding and control contributed to military coups becoming commonplace.

Barely ten years after Kwame Nkrumah had brought independence to Ghana—on February 24, 1966, to be precise—and five years after his friend Lumumba's assassination, Nkrumah left Ghana bound for Vietnam. Recognizing that the Vietnamese were fighting a war of independence like many African countries had successfully waged, Nkrumah was on his way to meet with Ho Chi Minh, the legendary nationalist leader who had been fighting a war of liberation—first against France, then against America—since the 1930s. On that fateful day, however, and serving as another warning shot across the bow of African independence, Nkrumah's government was overthrown by a military coup. Within the space of only a few days, Nkrumah had been ousted, parliament was dissolved, and suddenly Ghana was under the heel of a military dictatorship as ruthless as any colonial government of the past. British and US intelligence acted in collusion with the Ghanaian military in Nkrumah's removal from power. Over the next three decades, what happened that day in Ghana would repeat itself all over the African continent. Republic after republic, once laden with inordinate hopes, would crumble one by one, only to be replaced by ruthless military dictatorships supported either by the Soviet Union or the United States. Africa was once again locked in a death grip.

In the past, Western colonial powers had plundered Africa's shores, shipping out boatloads of ivory, gold, rubber, salt, and, of course, enslaved people. Today, Africa continues to be a cornucopia of wealth. Africa holds significant amounts of the world's supply of diamonds and gold, uranium, cobalt, bauxite, copper, and oil, and also houses covetous quantities of iron ore, chromium, manganese, titanium, and platinum. By the mid-twentieth century, these resources were the lifeblood of economies and governments around the world. Access to and control of these resources would become even more crucial during the Cold War, since uranium is used as a major source of energy and to make nuclear bombs, for example, and cobalt is needed to build fighter jets. Whoever controlled the resources of Africa would be that much nearer to winning the Cold War. And that meant controlling and influencing each and every one of Africa's fledgling governments.

3

AFRICA IN THE COLD WAR

Repression and Liberation

In this chapter, we take a look at how the Cold War is fought in Africa. While World War II was over by 1945, its epilogue was written worldwide by the Cold War, which derailed the dreams and potential of African independence. Perhaps the greatest tragedy of post-colonial Africa was how the United States and the Soviet Union's proxy conflict divided the continent along lines of global loyalty, and the newly independent African states were forced to take sides. In Africa, the Cold War was fought with guns and bombs; gunfire was heard from South Africa to Nigeria, from the Congo to Algeria. It brought to power a new breed of leader who received international support only so long as he did what the United States or the Soviet Union wanted, not necessarily what was best for his people or his nation. In South Africa this meant renewed Western support of apartheid, in Nigeria it meant coup after coup after coup, in the Congo it meant Mobutu Sese Seko, and in Algeria it meant the collapse of democratic hopes and possibilities. Across the continent, independence and democracy suffered. In this chapter, we define what the Cold War was and chart its impact on Africa, from the many coups all over the continent to European and American support for the apartheid fight against Southern African political independence.

THE COLD WAR

By the end of World War II, the United States was the clear economic and military victor. The economic infrastructures of Western Europe and Japan were damaged and weakened in the war, with the United States emerging as the most powerful economy the world had ever seen. This economic power reinforced the United States' efforts to exert its political interests worldwide. In addition to this newfound economic and political strength, the United States possessed nuclear weapons and the most powerful military force in the world. The United States responded to this new reality in two ways—exerting its economic might and engaging in a cold war with the Soviet Union.

With the defeat of Nazi Germany in 1945, so-called Greater Germany was divided into West Germany, East Germany, and Austria by the Allies. The war had a devastating impact on most European economies and infrastructures. Agreement between the Soviets and the Americans on a common solution to the post-war world did not materialize. These post-war considerations cut Europe in two and saved Western European capitalist society from the embrace of the Soviet Union. At any rate, by 1947 the world was plunged backward into a cold war. The Truman administration was confronted with Soviet unwillingness to collaborate on what to do with Germany after the war and on how to deal with the disorder caused by the destruction of Western Europe. The United States made the decision to drag Europe back into economic development and the capitalist system.

The Truman Doctrine, announced on March 12, 1947, was a program of military and economic assistance to Greece and Turkey, shortly thereafter extended to all US allies in Western Europe. In 1949 the North Atlantic Treaty Organization (NATO) was founded to safeguard the freedom and security of its members through political and military action. This system of collective defense offered member states mutual defense in response to attack by an external party. This was how the United States' new military power would cover Europe. Economic assistance came in the form of US secretary of state George C. Marshall's offer of aid and fair trade through the European Recovery Program. This is how the Truman Doctrine gave birth to the Marshall Plan and the Cold War.

US secretary of state George C. Marshall was concerned about the state of decline and disorder he witnessed in Western Europe after the war. He was also disappointed in the Soviet's unwillingness to collaborate on a German solution.[1] In April 1947, Marshall returned to the United States from a trip to Moscow and developed a plan for a European Recovery Program. Marshall publicly announced what would become known as the "Marshall Plan" during a 1947 commencement address at Harvard University. His agenda involved a path to recovery for Europe in which it would serve as a partner in a new, reinvigorated world economy of which the United States would be the clear and definitive leader. While the United States had already provided Europe with billions of dollars in grants and loans, up until the Marshall Plan, most of the grants and loans were used to meet emergencies and to provide essential supplies and repairs. By the spring of 1947, the trade deficit between Europe and the United States had grown to $4.742 billion.[2]

The Marshall Plan was fundamentally different as it was more a recovery and growth initiative than a disaster program. American advisers and specialists would continue to play prominent roles, with European governments deciding how to use the American aid for long-term investment and national reconstruction. Aid was confined to Western Europe, including Greece and Turkey, and ceased in 1952. In total, US aid to European reconstruction, culminating in the Marshall Plan, would be equivalent to more than $200 billion today. Politically, many in the US Congress saw the plan as an essential economic barrier to Soviet expansion and the "threat" of communism. In this way, the Marshall Plan was a response to the changing geopolitical landscape.

The Soviet Union declared its intention to gain a larger share of political and economic world power. In part this fight took place in the United Nations with debates about what would eventually become the 1948 Universal Declaration of Human Rights as well as the structure of the United Nations itself. The fight centered around the emphasis on two different types of human rights. So-called *first-generation human rights* emphasized civil and political rights. In contrast, the so-called *second-generation human rights* emphasized social, economic, and cultural rights to equality. Western Europe and the United States were champions of the first-generation human rights, while the Soviet Bloc, Africa, Asia, and Latin America tended to emphasize the second-generation human rights.[3]

After World War II, the Soviet Union experienced both an economic and military expansion that made it a true international political force. During this period, the Soviet Union supported "people's democracies" throughout Eastern Europe and the rest of the world. However, the contention over political and economic development was not always non-militaristic. The Soviet military occupation of Eastern Europe played a major role in countering the United States' threat to Soviet socialism, at least for a small period of time. Lines were being drawn, and tensions were on the rise. However, the Marshall Plan ensured rapid reconstruction, economic expansion, and a large share in the world's wealth for Western European countries, as well as for their ally, the United States.

Germany was the defeated world power. It was obvious to those in Moscow, Paris, London, and Washington that a post-war settlement in Germany was important to the future. Stalin asserted Soviet authority in

Eastern Europe and sought to gain an advantage in Germany. The Western allies met in London on June 1, 1948, and announced their plan to establish West Germany. Several weeks later, the new currency, the deutsche mark, was printed in the United States and shipped to Germany. A few days after the deutsche mark began circulation, the Soviet Union issued a new East German currency, the mark, and cut the rail lines connecting Berlin to Western Germany. Soviet troops tightened their control over the city, and the Western allies consolidated their part of Berlin. This crisis over Berlin produced two German states, required a significant military presence by the United States and the Soviet Union, and led to the creation of NATO and the Warsaw Treaty Organization of Friendship, Cooperation, and Mutual Assistance (the Warsaw Pact).

This tense situation developing between the dominant countries of the East and the West came to be known as the Cold War. This was the birth of a new international order. The old days of classical colonial domination of international commerce and politics ended with the successful German invasion of France in May 1940 and the entrance of the United States and the Soviet Union onto the world stage as saviors of the day. Following World War II, both the Soviet Union and the United States welcomed an end to colonialism in Asia and Africa to subvert the economic monopolies of the Western European colonial powers.

AFRICAN DECOLONIZATION AND REPRESSION

For different reasons, the Soviet Union and the United States politically encouraged the rise of nationalist movements in Asia and Africa. At first this support was reflected in the call of the two new superpowers for decolonization. Initially, France and Britain tried to respond by opening universities and lower-level schools and by increasing economic assistance and political participation, but these efforts were too little, too late. Africans had grown tired of colonialism, and such rule was of no use to either the United States or the Soviet Union. Ultimately, new approaches were undertaken, as World War II had undermined the myth of European invincibility.[4] The calls for decolonization by the United States and the Soviet Union did not mean liberation for Africa, and in fact the decolonization efforts by the new world powers contributed to the African-based forces of repression. In response, the African independence movements sought a way out of this cycle of external manipulations.

Anti-colonial nationalism became more militant in the 1940s and was accompanied by an interim period of internal self-government beginning in the early 1950s. Internal self-government in Africa offered a middle ground for negotiation on behalf of the colonial powers. For the nationalists, internal self-government offered an opportunity to develop organizationally. These processes led to more nationalists demanding independence and to an end of colonialism.

One of the first examples of this increased nationalism in the independence movement centered on the control of the Suez Canal. In Egypt, Egyptian army officers seized power in 1952, and the Egyptian king Farouk was deposed. Within a few years, former lieutenant colonel Gamal Abdel Nasser assumed leadership of the government by declaring himself Egypt's president in November of 1954. He pushed for the removal of British troops from Egyptian soil. At the time, Britain needed access to the Suez Canal and required Egyptian cooperation. The British were reliant on imported oil that was transported through the Suez Canal. If Egypt refused to cooperate with the British, the supply line would be disrupted, and Britain would have to use its precious dollars to buy oil elsewhere. Britain agreed—as it had promised dozens of times before—to withdraw from the Suez Canal. This time Britain followed through, and after seventy years of occupation, the last British troops withdrew from the Suez Canal on June 13, 1956.

The Cold War was in full effect, and all nations were supposed to take a side. Neutrality was not possible. Every country in the world had to align itself with either the Soviet Union or the United States. Nasser, the leader of Egypt, argued that the only solution for post-colonial countries lay in maintaining neutrality between the two superpowers. Indian prime minister Jawaharlal Nehru and Yugoslavian marshal Josip Broz Tito were also leading supporters of non-alignment. Nasser was a key player in the formation of the movement of independent states from Asia and Africa, which met at the historic Afro-Asian Conference in Bandung, Indonesia, from April 18 to 24, 1955. One of the first Asian and African conferences of newly independent states, the gathering was also known as the Bandung Conference. The twenty-nine participating countries represented a historic venture in the post–World War II era and expressed a collective voice of the world independence movement. The conference advocated Asian and African economic and cultural cooperation and opposed colonialism in any form. The Bandung Conference established a political solidarity among most of the states in Africa and Asia in the United Nations and fostered an

opportunity for economic cooperation among the members of the movement. By the time of the fifth conference, the Non-Aligned Movement had
grown to eighty-five nations that met in Colombo, Sri Lanka, under the
leadership of Indian prime minister Indira Gandhi. Here calls for a "new
world economic order" and "a revamping of the financial and currency
system" were reiterated.

In Cold War terms, Egypt was anything but non-aligned. After signing an arms deal in 1955 with the Soviet ally Czechoslovakia, Nasser soon
found himself in a confrontation with the West and its allies. In response to
Nasser and Nehru jointly issuing a "non-alignment" statement emphasiz-
ing a lack of dependence on the West on July 18, 1956, the United States
withdrew from talks regarding the possibility of financing the High Dam
at Aswan, a very large irrigation project. Nasser responded by nationalizing
the Suez Canal Company a week later. Given their financial and political
stakes in the canal, the French and British viewed this act as hostile. For
the Israelis, the nationalization of the Suez Canal Company opened up an
opportunity to move against a powerful and hostile neighboring state. At
a secret meeting, Britain, France, and Israel agreed to attack Egypt and
overthrow Nasser.

British, French, and Israeli forces landed in Suez in late 1956. In the
new Cold War world, this action was not only a threat to Egypt but also
to the United States and the Soviet Union. Cold War conflicts were no
longer to be resolved by the old colonial powers of Britain and France
unless in partnership with the United States. Times had changed, and war
was now viewed within the context of the strategic interests represented
by the United States in the Cold War against the Soviet Union. The two
opposing powers pressured the British, French, and Israelis to withdraw.
Nevertheless, Nasser's actions increased his reputation in both the colonial
and the post-colonial nations around the world, especially among Arab
countries and the colonies of Africa. Nasser was judged by popular opinion
to have been the political victor. Ultimately the Suez Crisis signaled to the
world that Britain could not maintain a global empire without superpower
support.[5]

Although the internal politics of Africa were heavily influenced by
the legacy of colonialism, the Cold War added another dimension. As the
British prime minister Harold Macmillan pointed out in his 1960 speech in
Cape Town, South Africa,

> As I see it the great issue in this second half of the twentieth century is
> whether the uncommitted peoples of Asia and Africa will swing to the

East or to the West. Will they be drawn into the Communist camp? Or will the great experiments in self-government that are now being made in Asia and Africa, especially within the Commonwealth, prove so successful, and by their example so compelling, that the balance will come down in favour of freedom and order and justice? The struggle is joined, and it is a struggle for the minds of men. What is now on trial is much more than our military strength or our diplomatic and administrative skill. It is our way of life.[6]

Macmillan's speech helps us understand how and why the Cold War would influence African politics. During the Cold War, in the East were the socialist countries led by the Soviet Union, and in the West were the capitalist countries led by the United States. The two world powers struggled for the hearts and minds, as well as the lives and resources, of the people in the contested zones of Asia, Africa, and South America.

In 1961, with aid from the Soviet Union, the German Democratic Republic (also known as East Germany), built the Berlin Wall. The wall completely cut off West Berlin from surrounding East Berlin and East Germany. For many, the Berlin Wall symbolized the "iron curtain" separating the capitalist West from the socialist East.[7] Around the world, the voice of US president John F. Kennedy was heard as he proclaimed in his June 26, 1963, speech in West Berlin,

> There are some who say that Communism is the wave of the future. Let them come to Berlin. And there are some who say in Europe and elsewhere we can work with the Communists. Let them come to Berlin. And there are even a few who say that it's true that Communism is an evil system, but it permits us to make economic progress. "Laßt sie nach Berlin kommen." Let them come to Berlin!
>
> Freedom has many difficulties and democracy is not perfect, but we have never had to put a wall up to keep our people in, to prevent them from leaving us.[8]

Kennedy's words rung loudly because they were spoken just twenty-two months after Soviet-backed East Germany erected the Berlin Wall to prevent mass emigration. A very notable moment during the Cold War, Kennedy's speech marked the significance of this war for everyone. His comments were directed as much at the Soviet Union as at the East German government.

Kennedy's words were spoken in 1963, but the Cold War began as soon as World War II ended. It was the crisis in the Congo that came to represent the Cold War's arrival in Africa, and it reflects how Cold War events in Africa impacted the world.

PATRICE LUMUMBA'S CONGO

By 1960, millions of Congolese people had been exterminated under Belgian King Leopold's pillaging and plundering, followed by the extreme policies of the Belgian government over the next seventy-five years. The greed and brutal colonial reign of terror perpetrated by King Leopold became a symbol of genocidal colonial violence in Africa. Mark Twain's *King Leopold's Soliloquy* was published in 1905 as a political satire that harshly condemns the brutal acts of King Leopold in the Congo.

> But enough of trying to tally off his crimes! His list is interminable, we should never get to the end of it. His awful shadow lies across his Congo Free State, and under it an unoffending nation of 15,000,000 is withering away and swiftly succumbing of their miseries. It is a land of graves; it is The Land of Graves; it is the Congo Free Graveyard. It is a majestic thought: that is, this ghastliest episode in all human history is the work of one man alone; one solitary man; just a single individual—Leopold, King of the Belgians. He is personally and solely responsible for all the myriad crimes that have blackened the history of the Congo State. He is sole master there; he is absolute. He could have prevented the crimes by his mere command; he could stop them today with a word. He withholds the word. For his pocket's sake.[9]

King Leopold's murderous legacy includes over ten million African deaths and millions of victims of the torturous colonial rule of Belgium. Images of the severed limbs of those who did not meet their quotas of rubber became international symbols of colonial brutality.[10] No one needed freedom more than the long-suffering Congolese. What they did not know was that freedom would be granted with undesirable conditions attached.

Patrice Lumumba was a close ally of Kwame Nkrumah and a fellow compatriot in the Pan-African movement. The son of a farmer, Lumumba came of age during a pivotal period in African history. As a journalist for Congolese news magazines, he saw firsthand how much the Congo was in need of radical change. Lumumba cofounded the Mouvement National Congolais (MNC) in the late 1950s. Using Gandhi's techniques of strikes and demonstrations, Lumumba and others led the march to independence against Belgium's colonial rule. On June 23, 1960, Congo declared its independence from Belgium, and thirty-four-year-old Lumumba became Congo's first democratically elected prime minister.

This was a great moment for the Congo and the African independence movement. Yet the Congo, like other African states, was not fully prepared to grapple with the international politics of independence. Contrary to the newsreels, messages, and propaganda from the Belgian government, at the time of independence there were fewer than thirty African university graduates and no Congolese army officers, engineers, or physicians. Belgians had dominated the colony's civil service, with less than five of the five thousand administrative positions filled by Africans.

King Baudouin of Belgium arrived in Leopoldville to officially grant the Congo its independence on June 30, 1960. His arrival was met with great fanfare, and even Lumumba himself was in the receiving line to welcome the king. So, with great horror, he and his colleagues listened to King Baudouin's speech, which included paternalistic statements such as "It is now up to you gentlemen to show that you are worthy of our confidence" and "Don't compromise the future with hasty reforms, and don't replace the structures that Belgium hands over to you until you are sure you can do better." In response, Lumumba was "seen desperately scribbling a new speech to answer that of the king." When delivering it, he was interrupted several times by applause from the Congolese in attendance and given an ovation at the end:

> No Congolese worthy of the name can ever forget that it is by struggle that we have won [our independence], a struggle waged each and every day, a passionate idealistic struggle, a struggle in which no effort, privatization, suffering, or drop of our blood was spared. . . . We have known sarcasm and insults, endured blows morning, noon and night, because we were "niggers." Who will forget that a Black was addressed in the familiar "tu," not as a friend, but because the polite "vous" was reserved for Whites only? We have seen our lands despoiled under the terms of what was supposedly the law of the land but which only recognised the right of the strongest. We have seen that this law was quite different for a White than for a Black: accommodating for the former, cruel and inhuman for the latter. We have seen the terrible suffering of those banished to remote regions because of their political opinions or religious beliefs; exiled within their own country, their fate was truly worse than death itself. . . . And, finally, who can forget the volleys of gunfire in which so many of our brothers perished, the cells where the authorities threw those who would not submit to a rule where justice meant oppression and exploitation?[11]

Patrice Lumumba, first prime minister of the Democratic Republic of the Congo, and members of his government, 1960. Screenshot from *African Independence*.

The glory of the moment would be short lived. The Congo quickly descended into political chaos as an untested government struggled to hold together a country the size of Europe that had never known democratic rule. For example, less than seven months after the declaration of independence, the mining region of Katanga declared its independence from the Congo under the leadership of Moïse Tshombe with support from the Belgian government and the Union Minière mining company. By this time, the United Nations had troops on the ground in the Congo, but they refused to help suppress the rebellion. In response, Lumumba sought assistance from the Soviet Union and other independent African states.

Furthermore, political rifts grew between Lumumba and the Congo's military leaders, including Joseph-Desire Mobutu. A former soldier in the old colonial Force Publique, Mobutu had joined Lumumba's MNC in the 1950s and served as his assistant in that organization. In his capacity as Lumumba's assistant, Mobutu gained an international reputation as a very competent individual, and he fostered relationships with Belgium and US diplomats. Upon independence, he became the army chief of staff of the new nation. He gained this position because of his close political relationship with Lumumba. However, Mobutu, with US and Belgium encouragement, eventually staged a coup in 1965 and held power for decades.

In addition to these local and international conspirators, behind the scenes of the coup and Lumumba's execution lurked the formidable shadow of the United States and the Central Intelligence Agency (CIA). On August 26, 1960, the director of the CIA, Allen Dulles, cabled his agents in the Congo a message about Lumumba that read, "We conclude that his removal must be an urgent and prime objective and that under existing conditions that should be a high priority of our covert action."[12]

About a month later, on September 24, 1960, Dulles cabled CIA agents in the Congo, stating, "We wish give every possible support in eliminating Lumumba from any possibility resuming governmental position." On December 2, 1960, the United Nations transferred Lumumba to Mobutu's troops. Just six months after having led Congo to independence, Lumumba was arrested and brutally beaten by Congolese soldiers. A month and a half later, after forced imprisonment and torture, thirty-five-year-old Patrice Lumumba, as well as his close political colleagues, former vice president of the Senate Joseph Okito and sports and youth minister Maurice Mpolo, were secretly shot to death by a firing squad composed of Belgian military police and police from the Katanga. The complicity of the Belgian and US governments in Lumumba's assassination is now openly recognized.[13]

The first prime minister of the DRC, Patrice Lumumba (right); Joseph Okito (center); and Maurice Mpolo (left), arrested and tortured, 1961. Screenshot from *African Independence*.

Newsreels during that time show reactions to the brutal murders of Lumumba, Okito, and Mpolo. Their deaths were met with protests around the world. The Soviet Union demanded the dismissal of United Nations secretary general Dag Hammarskjöld, who justified the acts of the United Nations. Also calling for the resignation of Hammarskjöld were hundreds who picketed outside the United Nations in New York City on February 15, 1960; attempting to march on Times Square, demonstrators were dispersed by police. Many of the protestors went to Harlem later that evening for a rally.[14] In the midst of this international outrage, US ambassador to the United Nations, Adlai Stevenson, addressed the Soviet Union's demand in his February 15, 1960, address to the UN Security Council,

> We believe that the only way to keep the cold war out of the Congo is to keep the United Nations in the Congo, and we call on the Soviet Union to join us in thus ensuring the free and untrammeled exercise by the Congolese people of their right to independence and to democracy. . . . It is the security of all peoples which is threatened by the statement and by the proposal of the Soviet Government.[15]

The hypocrisy of the position of the United States is evident in comparing the CIA cables to its agents in the field and the US ambassador's statements in the United Nations. This would not be the last time that the United States used the United Nations as a political tool in its international politics of intervention and political subversion. The Congo's coup d'état took place during the heart of the Cold War era. Global politics had become a chess match with two powerful adversaries competing against one another: the US and the USSR. And in the case of Lumumba, behind the scenes of the coup and his execution lurked the formidable shadow of the United States and the CIA.

The sentiment among those supporting African independence was decisively opposed to this outside intervention. At the time, K. B. Asante was Kwame Nkrumah's personal assistant. Frequently making trips around Africa, he worked with George Padmore, under Nkrumah's direction, to foster a more Pan-African vision among African leaders. Asante provides a unique perspective regarding these events. He talked to me about their significance and the Cold War connections.

> It was the richest country, and if the Congo had been allowed to develop with Lumumba and some of the people who thought like him, it could have been a great country and it would have stabilized the middle of Africa and helped a great deal. But now it's a place where

what happens? All sorts of crimes . . . have been committed by soldiers, by politicians. It's terrible. And then Mobutu was forced on them, and he robbed the country.

So it became a Cold War, only in the UN offices and so, but in the actual practice, it was a question of a dominated country with leaders who were promoting Western ideas.

The United States continued to support Mobutu and other African dictators throughout the Cold War. In August 1970, Mobutu traveled to Washington, D.C., as the first African head of state to be welcomed by President Richard Nixon.[16] On the south lawn of the White House, President Nixon made the following welcoming remarks to Mobutu:

> Mr. President, it is a special privilege for me to welcome you today to the White House. You are a young leader of a young country. In fact, the Congo is the youngest country of all those that have been represented by state visits since I have been President of this country.
>
> I have the privilege of knowing your country and of knowing your people, and I can tell the American people that while your country is young—only 10 years of age—that it has had a period of progress in that period which has been an example for nations throughout the world.
>
> You have moved forward economically, you have established unity in your country, and you have a vitality, which impresses every visitor when he comes to the Congo.
>
> I have been looking forward to this visit so that the people of the United States could know you and, through you, know your people and your country. . . . The Congo is a good investment not only because of its natural wealth but because of a wealth even more important than its natural resources, a strong and vigorous and progressive people, and a stable leadership.[17]

Mobutu responded to Nixon's remarks by making it clear that support from the United States was vital to his regime's survival:

> I will tell you when we meet later to explore the bilateral questions between the United States and the Democratic Republic of the Congo, but I should like to tell you now also that in coming here I bring you a message from the people of the Congo, a message to your people, to thank you for the aid that the American people have given to my country for the last 10 years. There is a saying in my country that it is in times of need that you know your friends and, indeed, the United States has stood by us and this we shall never forget.[18]

Congolese president Mobutu Sese Seko and President Richard Nixon at the White House in 1970. Screenshot from *African Independence*.

SOUTHERN AFRICA

Southern Africa provides another context for understanding what needs to be seen as the Cold War on Africa. In fact, in the 1970s, the South African government was leading the Western fight in the Cold War on the African continent, especially in the Southern African region. The independence movements in Angola, Mozambique, South-West Africa, Rhodesia, and South Africa found support from the Soviet Union, China, Cuba, and the bordering "frontline states." The South African government found itself fighting communism in these very same nations. The efforts of the South African government contributed to the creation of a counterforce by the newly independent frontline states of Angola, Botswana, Lesotho, Mozambique, Tanzania, Zambia, and Zimbabwe. The frontline states organized efforts to achieve democratic rule in South Africa and were responsible for several significant peace agreements, including those between South Africa and Angola (the Lusaka Protocol), Mozambique, and Namibia (the New York Accords).

In April 1969, President Kenneth Kaunda hosted a meeting of non-aligned states that produced the Lusaka Manifesto, which called for majority rule. The manifesto was adopted by the Organization of African Unity and was defended by African presidents of Botswana, the Cameroon, and others at the United Nations.[19] Kenneth Kaunda explained to me the context in which this decision was made:

> Our colleagues all came back from Tanganyika to Zambia because we were nearer to their places: to Angola, to Mozambique, to Zimbabwe, to Namibia, to South Africa. We were nearer to those places. So they had to come to Zambia, and we had a duty. Love thy neighbor as thou lovest thyself. Do unto others as you would have them do unto you. We had a duty to do unto them how we would have liked them to do unto us. We allowed them to come.
>
> Young man, that is how South Africa is now what it is. In Angola, Mozambique, South Africans in South Africa, and the British particulars in Zimbabwe, they started bombing our Zambia. They destroyed our bridges; they did all sorts of dirty things against us.

Indeed, as wars for independence continued, the colonial governments of Rhodesia and South Africa attacked areas in Zambia because of its continuous support for African political independence. Kaunda, president at that time, explained why Zambia made such a tremendous sacrifice:

> We understood. We are helping our colleagues to end their struggle. But in the end, thank God, thank God, our Creator, they succeeded, with our help, humble help. They won. That's what happened.

Interview with Kenneth Kaunda, first president of Zambia (1964–1991), 2010. Screenshot from *African Independence.*

In an interview with the *Herald* on April 8, 1980, a journalist asked President Kenneth Kaunda about the cost to Zambia of the Zimbabwe liberation war and when he expected to restore the Zambian economy to stability. He responded,

> The United Nations put it at about K1 billion. When we think in terms of what we have not done which we should have done it's incalculable. But whatever we have lost, it was worth it. It was a price worth paying and we are proud to have paid it.

I asked President Benjamin Mkapa, third president of the United Republic of Tanzania, from 1995 to 2005, to share his thoughts on the impact of the Cold War on African independence:

> The Cold War prolonged the subjugation of the majority of the people of southern Africa because the colonial authorities, for instance in Zimbabwe and certainly the governments of South Africa and Namibia, presented themselves as the defenders of Western civilization, Western values, against this horrible communist, communist regimes of Eastern Europe. And they supported one another to suppress the legitimate nationalist aspirations of the people of southern Africa. So that was one effect of the Cold War, but then after we were able to decouple ourselves from domination by the West, then it was almost an understood precondition that we would side with them if it came to disputes with the communist countries.
>
> There were some who were very strong in saying, "No, we will be non-aligned," non-aligned in respect of West and East, but those were very few. In large measure we were dragged into supporting the Western point of view even as newly independent countries, so that also retarded our process of self-realization, if you like, politically as well as economically.
>
> And then finally when that Cold War broke, but even before, before the fall of the wall, even before then, in the process of ensuring that we lined up with the Western countries, these countries were not loathe to put it mildly to see regimes that were asserting themselves more independently overthrown. And that is one of the explanations for the many military coups of the 1960s and '70s. Remember, there were coups almost every other month in Africa.

President Benjamin Mkapa during interview, 2012. Screenshot from *African Independence*.

COUP AFTER COUP

The influence of US strategic interests on Africa often took the form of a coup, as was the case of Ghana under Kwame Nkrumah. During and after independence in 1957, Ghana was a close friend of the United States. Newsreels show Vice President Richard Nixon leading a high-level delegation from the United States to the independence celebrations in 1957. In March 1961, they also show Nkrumah and his entourage being greeted at the airport by then president John F. Kennedy shortly after gaining independence. However, as independence in Ghana developed, Nkrumah became a vocal advocate for socialism in Africa. Nkrumah had always indicated his support for socialism; however, he increasingly became openly anti-capitalist and developed closer ties with the Soviet Union and China. Increasingly, Nkrumah's Pan-Africanism was seen as a threat to the Cold War intentions of the United States.

Given Nkrumah's longtime association with Ho Chi Minh (an attendee at the Fifth Pan-African Congress and a prominent attendee at the Asian-African Bandung Conference in 1955 in Indonesia), it is not surprising that he would call on Nkrumah in his time of need. In 1966, Nkrumah was on his way to Hanoi at the invitation of President Ho Chi Minh. He was carrying with him proposals for ending the war in Vietnam. When Nkrumah's flight landed in China, Lieutenant General J. A. Ankrah announced that Nkrumah was no longer the head of state in Ghana. The Cold War, especially the British and US intelligence forces, had removed Africa's strongest voice for independence and Pan-Africanism from power. The celebrations in Ghana at the time of his fall marked Ghana's entrance into the business of coup after coup after coup. The forces opposed to Nkrumah's Pan-Africa aims gained power on the international stage, and the Organization of African Unity (OAU) became more of a voice for moderation and border consolidation and less of a voice for African unification.

By 1974, Ethiopia also found itself caught in the grip of Cold War politics. Chapter 1 began with Ethiopia having caught the eye of the fascist government in Italy. During World War II, Ethiopia defeated the second Italian effort to place it within the orbit of Italy's strategic interests.

In the years following the end of World War II, opposition to the rule of Emperor Haile Selassie grew. This opposition turned into a civil war, this war turned into a coup, and this coup witnessed Eritrean independence. It was here in 1974 that Mengistu Haile Mariam seized control of Ethiopia's government through a military coup and created a one-party socialist state. Mengistu was the most prominent officer in the Derg, the communist military junta that seized power and governed the country. Mengistu was the president of the newly named People's Democratic Republic of Ethiopia from 1987 to 1991.

Under the Derg, Ethiopia quickly became a political nightmare. Mengistu immediately expelled the Americans who had originally held sway over the previous government, driving out their military missions and severing diplomatic ties. In Washington, Mengistu's photo now took a prominent place on the "enemy" list. Consistent with the Cold War practices of the day, under Mengistu's reign, Ethiopia received aid from the Soviet Union and other Warsaw Pact members, as well as from Cuba. Ethiopia was considered a strategic country by both the United States and the Soviet Union given its large population of over forty million people as well as its close proximity to the Red Sea.[20]

Between 1977 and 1978, in the midst of Ethiopia's civil war, Mengistu's government instituted a new policy of nationwide purges, apprehending, torturing, and executing suspected political opponents and many of the country's intellectuals. Often this simply meant anyone studying at the university, as higher education was considered a suspect activity. Those who weren't tortured and killed were prevented from studying and instead were forced to work in remote parts of the country, allegedly to help "educate" the peasants. Ethiopia began a descent into a period of nearly constant civil war, one that would ultimately take the lives of an estimated two million people. As the Cold War was about to end, and following seventeen years of fighting the Tigrian Liberation Front, Mengistu fled to Zimbabwe in May 1991. The civil war in Sudan was also directly caught up with the war going on in Ethiopia as Numeri was a US ally, but John Garang's Sudanese People's Liberation Army (SPLA) became allied with Mengistu.

AFRICAN POWER IN THE COLD WAR

In a previous conversation with His Excellency John Kufuor, president of the Fourth Republic of Ghana from 2001 to 2009, he made a very strong statement about the Cold War and the sides that were selected by various leaders. He said, "A lot of the leaders were forced by the Cold War to side with ideologies and policies they really didn't understand, and in the process, they led their people into the confusion that prevailed in those times."

When asked to elaborate, President Kufuor continued:

> I will still stand by that. You see, the movements towards independence were led by freedom fighters. They were good in rallying their people around to demand independence and freedom from colonial masters, and they succeeded. But being good at rallying people to break free and loose of bondage does not automatically make you a good economic performer or manager. And because they lacked the preparation for that, many of them, practically all of them, they failed. In the process, too, they had come, one way or the other, under the influences of the Cold War. The Cold War meant you are either with the West or with the East and these two sides fighting for hegemony around the globe. They didn't allow these primary leaders to at least observe and to decide. Time you were independent, dependent on the strategic interests of the former master, colonial master, so they divided the world. You came under the influences of the divide.

The push to have newly independent African governments choose between the strategic interests of the capitalist West and the socialist East was so intense because so much was at stake. Africa was not a side player in the Cold War. Africa was a central player. In a way, Africa held the resources necessary to play in the Cold War.

For another specific example, I asked President Kenneth Kaunda about the impact of the Cold War on his politics in Zambia at the time. He replied,

> I was in power from 1964 to 1991. How do you do that? How do you manage that? We had many parties. Then we become independent. Many parties were still there. But I knew very well that if we did not handle this thing carefully, our own independence would be undermined and destroyed. What do I mean?
>
> The Portuguese in Angola, Portuguese in Mozambique, the settlers, the British settlers in Zimbabwe, the British and the Boer settlers in South Africa and in Namibia, the German settlers there, would all gang up against us and would upset our government. So we had to think of something else. So we began talking to our colleagues, different parties. I explained to them, if we don't handle this thing, our own independence will be destroyed, undermined. Let's come together. And so long as South Africa is there, Angola is there under the Portuguese, Zimbabwe is there under the British, now Mozambique is there under the Portuguese— these people would join hands with a number of our own Zambians, and their party, different parties, to upset us. They understood. So in the end, we came to, or we agreed, one party, participatory democracy.
>
> We went through the country talking to people. We were . . . we passed a great campaign in the country, explaining what was happening. So we said, if, when in the future, if we want to go back to multi-partyism, we would again go around and asking people whether they wanted us to go back to multi-party, at another stage.

President Kaunda clarified how the national referendum gave him the mandate to stay in power as long as he did. In his view, the Cold War and the persistence of colonialism in Southern Africa were the reasons for his longevity in office.

> I held the power the way I did because we had people who were bombing us. Those were enemies of democracy, enemies of Zambia, because Zambia supported freedom fighters.

For a perspective from another generation of African politicians, I asked Ghanaian politician Samia Nkrumah about the role the Cold War played in African politics.

> Yes. Very, very, I think, terrible. Because I think more than other places, African countries have been victims—Africa as a whole has been

a victim of the Cold War. Because we are made up of all these small states, which are unviable economically, and we've lost, many leaders, nationalistic leaders, patriotic, who in the course of trying to advance their countries economically have turned to the East as much as they have turned to the West. But because of that, they paid a heavy price, and they were eliminated or compromised. So we've lost great leaders because of the Cold War. So I think it's had a terrible impact on African countries.

The Cold War rhetoric about freedom versus totalitarianism was bloody for many of the people in Africa. In fact, this rhetoric was not reality. The Cold War was far bloodier on the African continent than the fight for African independence, and it has had a fundamental impact on how African independence has been perceived by the rest of the world.

APARTHEID

The people and the independence movement in South Africa were particularly hard hit by Cold War geopolitics. Six weeks after Prime Minister Macmillan's speech in Cape Town calling for a change in the South African government policies of apartheid, protests occurred throughout the country on March 21, 1960. Police responded with gunfire. In Sharpeville and

South Africans burning their passbooks following the brutal Sharpeville and Langa massacres in 1960. Screenshot from *African Independence*.

nearby Vanderbijlpark, as well as in Langa outside of Cape Town, an estimated seventy people were killed and hundreds were injured. The South African government also declared a state of emergency and banned several political organizations. This was not the first massacre under the South African regime. However this time images of protesters being brutalized and shot were circulated in the global media.[21]

I spoke with South African politician Prince Inkosi Mangosuthu Buthelezi, whose uncle, Dr. Pixley Ka Isaka Seme, founded the African National Congress (ANC). In 1911, he had argued in an article entitled "Native Union" that "We are one people. These divisions, these jealousies, are the cause of all our woes and of all our backwardness and ignorance today." The article was published in several newspapers and is considered one of the ANC's founding documents. His call for unity led to the creation of what would become the ANC. The ANC was formed at a time of economic boom in South Africa, and everything was changing quickly. The gold mining industry was growing in the early twentieth century and led to increasing wealth in what was then known as the Union of South Africa. Gold exports drove the economy. Laws and taxes were used to force African people off their land and to make them dependent on the white farm and mine owners. The 1913 Land Act went so far as to prevent Africans from owning, renting, or even using land except in certain parts of the country. By the 1950s and 1960s, the ANC was transformed into a mass movement for political independence. Prince Buthelezi was a member of the ANC in the 1960s. In his Durban office, I asked him about the significance of the Sharpeville and Langa uprisings.

> Of course, it was really the biggest tragedy and probably the turning point, you know, in the struggle, which as mooted by the founders of the ANC was supposed to be a peaceful struggle. And they decided that the future would be negotiated around the conference table. But I think that was the climax, you know, of the human rights violations that had been perpetrated against our people for many generations, when the Sharpeville tragedy took place.
>
> And I remember that after that, the leader of the ANC at the time was Inkosi Albert Luthuli. I remember that, after that, only then they were prompted by the tragedy to burn their own passes.
>
> And, of course, the person who was really responsible for that demonstration was actually Robert Sobukwe of the Pan-African Congress [PAC], who had been our chairperson of the youth league when he was still in the ANC as well. So he had a great impact on all of us. Even though when he halved off to found the PAC, I remained in the ANC

Prince Inkosi Mangosuthu Buthelezi, South African politician at his office in Durban, South Africa, 2008. Screenshot from *African Independence*.

myself, but still, I mean, I still admired him, I mean, to the end of his days, for his contribution.

Prince Buthelezi also later broke off from the ANC and ultimately formed his own political organization.

I had a conversation with a representative from the Pan-African Congress, one of the leading organizations in the fight against apartheid. The PAC was a politically significant organization in the South African struggle for liberation in the 1970s and 1980s. I met with the representative in Cape Town's District Six. This location was a major site in the political struggle against apartheid. In 1966, the South African government declared District Six a whites-only district under the 1950 Group Areas Act. Black and colored populations were evicted en masse. Less than two decades later, over fifty thousand people were relocated from District Six to a dilapidated suburb of Cape Town, Cape Flats, and had their homes demolished.

To get a sense of the day-to-day activities of political struggle in District Six during this time, I spoke with Dr. Sedick Isaacs before he passed away in 2012. Isaacs had been a member of the PAC and a freedom fighter for the political liberation of South Africa. He had spent thirteen years at the infamous Robben Island prison alongside Nelson Mandela and others.[22]

Remember the times, of the late '50s early '60s, when people were wanting action and activity, and during that time the ANC was regarded

Interview with Dr. Sedick Isaacs, a member of the Pan-African Congress, in Durban, South Africa, 2008. Screenshot from *African Independence*.

as a bit of a lame organization, and the PAC had energy and determination and they started organizing. And, you know, there was also this "pass" protest they had, and one, the thing that really impressed people, the PAC, was the march from Langa. They had a protest march, and thousands of people from Langa started marching through to the city center. It created panic amongst the government and the police. But it created admiration from all of us, and that's why we thought that it was the organization to go for.

We were getting tired of all these meetings and protests and saying that we have been treated like this, and we've been treated like this, and excluded from that, and we thought, well, talking must end sooner or later, and we need to get into something more positive.

What did you do in the Pan-African Congress?

Well, at that time, I was really just a member at the ordinary level. But I was interested in seeing how other people . . . they say, "How other people lived"; we thought you should say, "How other people died." And we started at Langa in the black areas, although it was illegal to enter. You could be arrested and also charged for entering the areas of blacks. But we went there. But my interest at that time was explosives. I did a degree in chemistry, and I was particularly interested in explosives, and I taught the use and manufacture of explosives from ordinary living material. At that time, I was also interested in other forms of offensive weapons, like offensive gasses that could go in and disable areas without necessarily killing people, and then you can do whatever you want to afterwards. And things like a castor oil as a component for gases. Of course castor oil is very poisonous, and that was my interest.

Who did you teach to make explosives?

I was teaching at the school, just around the corner here, called Trafalgar High School. And that was my part-time occupation. The other one was experimentations with explosives, politics, and various discussions.

In fact, the school was already active; it was a center of political activity, even before I came there. And although the government and the court tried to make believe that I was the troublemaker . . . the school was already very actively involved.

Now, why were you arrested?

Well, for teaching—for handling the explosives. They couldn't get to the teaching part of it. I remember at that time, the government could merely certify that you are guilty of terrorism, sabotage, and you got to prove yourself innocent. And they had a certificate against me, and I was detained in terms of this detention without trial.

Prisons have always been used as an option in political struggles over the power of the state. South Africa was not an exception to this general practice. In fact, South Africa was home to the most significant political prisoner in history.

Considered the father of the anti-apartheid movement and an international icon in the struggle for political independence, freedom, and justice, Nelson Mandela was a leader of the African National Congress. A founding member of the organization's youth league, Mandela rose rapidly through the ranks and developed a following within the ANC due to his more radical policies. By 1960 he was one of the ANC's main leaders. After a brief stint on trial and in prison for fighting against the apartheid regime, he went into exile, traveled around the African continent, and received military training before returning to continue in the fight against apartheid. In his first television interview, given in 1961, he defined the fight against apartheid as part of the independence movement.

The Africans require, want, the franchise on the basis of one man, one vote. They want political independence. We have made it very clear in our policy, that South Africa is a country of many races. There is room for all the various races in this country.

First-known interview of Nelson Mandela in 1960. Screenshot from *African Independence*.

He also discussed the possibility of more militant tactics: "If the government reaction is to crush by naked force our non-violent demonstrations, we will have to seriously reconsider our tactics. In my mind, we are closing a chapter on this question of non-violent policy."[23]

A few years after making this statement, Nelson Mandela was incarcerated, and his imprisonment on Robben Island became legendary. While Mandela was incarcerated, a new generation of activists took to the streets in South Africa during the 1970s. Steve Biko was the leading voice of this era and is considered the father of the black consciousness movement. In 1973 the South African government banned him from traveling, speaking in public, or writing for publications. By then, the black consciousness movement was inspiring youth and translating into political action.

To get a firsthand account of this political action, I met with Mbuso Chili, one of the former students who participated in the Biko-inspired 1976 Soweto Uprising, which shook the world with protest against apartheid.[24]

As I described to Chili, in 1976, I was going to be in my senior year in high school, and I remember June of that year being a very hot month.

Yes, here, it is cold here.

Interview with Mbuso Chili, a student activist leader in Soweto, 2012. Screenshot from *African Independence*.

South Africa in 1976 was very cold, and where I was, it was very hot. That year I heard about schoolchildren who had shaken South Africa, and it really made me wonder, what's going on there?

> What happened is, the apartheid government, they wanted to introduce Afrikaans as a medium language. They wanted us to do math in Afrikaans. They wanted us to do other studies in Afrikaans.

So what was wrong with learning biology, math, and social sciences in Afrikaans?

> The oppression, you understand, because here these people, they came to our country, they took over, and they want to control us. To me that was an oppression. They want to enforce something that we did not want.

Okay, if I'm standing here in the heart of Soweto, 16th of June, 1976, what do I see?

> You'd see black here. You'd see black. As they say, black is beautiful. You will see black, every, every, each and every student. Everybody was here.
>
> As everybody was coming to gather here, the police started to come, started to come around. So they wanted us to disperse. Because they said, this was illegal gathering.

Memorial to Hector Pieterson, a student who was brutally killed during the 1976 Soweto Uprising in South Africa, 2012. Screenshot from *African Independence*.

One of the tragedies of the Soweto uprising was the shooting of thirteen-year-old Hector Pieterson, one of the first casualties of state repression against the protestors.[25]

So how was Hector Pieterson shot?

> Hector Pieterson was shot because he was following [his] sister. So [his] sister apparently wasn't aware that Hector Pieterson was following her, you understand. So when he got to this street, [his] sister realized that Hector Pieterson was following her. That's when the scuffle broke, you understand. . . . [The police] are speaking with these loudspeakers. You have got two minutes to disperse, and all that, you understand. And then everything started to be chaotic.
>
> [The police] started shooting randomly, you understand, without any provocation. They started shooting randomly. That's how Hector Pieterson was shot. In fact I think he was shot at close range.

Shot at close range.

Yes.

Biko, who had inspired the Soweto uprising and who remains a symbol of African independence movements, was brutally murdered while in police custody on September 12, 1977. In an interview with a European journalist, Biko offered an explanation for the political unrest and discussed the organization "Black People's Convention" (BPC), which he cofounded in 1972:

> The primary reason behind the unrest is simple lack of patience by the young folk with a government, which is refusing to change, refusing the change in the educational sphere, which is where they [the students] are directing themselves, and also refusing to change in a broader political situation.
>
> And for black people to be able to work out a programme they needed to defeat the one main element in politics, which was working against them: a psychological feeling of inferiority, which was deliberately cultivated by the system. So equally, too, the whites in order to be able to listen to blacks needed to defeat the one problem, which they had, which was one of "superiority." . . .
>
> Now the only way to come about this of course was to look anew at the black man in terms of what it is in him that is lending him to denigration so easily. . . .
>
> Now the line BPC adopts is to explore as much as possible non-violent means within the country, and that is why we exist.
>
> But there are people—and there are many people—who have despaired of the efficacy of non-violence as a method. They are of the view that the present Nationalist Government can only be unseated by people operating a military wing.

Steve Biko, leader in the South African independence movement, circa 1977. Screenshot from *African Independence*.

I don't know if this is the final answer. I think in the end there is going to be a totality of the effect of a number of change agencies operating in South Africa. I personally would like to see fewer groups. I would like to see groups like ANC, PAC and the Black Consciousness Movement deciding to form one liberation group.[26]

Cracks in the armor of the South African feelings of superiority began to be reflected in international changes in the dynamics of the Cold War. Speaking at the United Nations on September 24, 1984, President Ronald Reagan outlined the US policy toward South Africa:

The United States considers it a moral imperative that South Africa's racial policies evolve peacefully but decisively toward a system compatible with basic norms of justice, liberty, and human dignity. I'm pleased that American companies in South Africa, by providing equal employment opportunities, are contributing to the economic advancement of the black population. But clearly, much more must be done. . . .

The United States has been and will always be a friend of peaceful solutions. This is no less true with respect to my country's relations with the Soviet Union.

When I appeared before you last year, I noted that we cannot count on the instinct for survival alone to protect us against war. Deterrence is necessary but not sufficient. America has repaired its strength. We have invigorated our alliances and friendships. We are ready for constructive negotiations with the Soviet Union.

We recognize that there is no sane alternative to negotiations on arms control and other issues between our two nations which have the capacity to destroy civilization as we know it. I believe this is a view shared by virtually every country in the world and by the Soviet Union itself. And I want to speak to you today on what the United States and the Soviet Union can accomplish together in the coming years and the concrete steps that we need to take.[27]

This policy of "constructive engagement" linked US support for the apartheid regime to the fight against communism. In South Africa, the fight against communism included several battles with Cuban troops in Angola. In fact, the Cuban victory on the battlefield against the apartheid forces was important in bringing the South African government to the negotiation table. And Cuban support for the struggle against the apartheid regime was decisive in the Angolan War. I asked Pik Botha, who served as the foreign minister of South Africa in the last years of apartheid, about this strange relationship.

In general, the activities of the Soviet Union were feared, particularly as they entered into a certain region somewhere in the world and start causing problems. You've got it in Korea, in Vietnam, elsewhere, right around Afghanistan; and so here in South Africa, being isolated from Europe and the rest of the so-called developed world at the time—relatively developed—there was a very great fear for years that drove the electorate here and the government to adopt very strict laws against communism, and were considering movements like the ANC and others almost as a communist threat too, to life—a normal life here in South Africa. So the Cold War had that—had that effect here. It animated and strengthened those in South Africa who warned against communist infiltration and aggression.

On June 12, 1987, during the 750th anniversary of the city of Berlin, President Reagan called for an end to the Cold War in his remarks on East-West relations, delivered at the Brandenburg Gate in West Berlin. His speech was symbolic in many ways because it issued a challenge to the Soviet Union and the country's leader, Mikhail Gorbachev, to destroy the Berlin Wall. The speech also served as a call to end the Cold War. USSR president Mikhail Gorbachev had expressed a desire to increase freedom in the Eastern Bloc through his policies of *glasnost* and *perestroika*. These two policies were seen as efforts by the Soviet Union to increase the transparency of its government by restructuring its bureaucratic processes. In his speech, President Reagan said,

> There is one sign the Soviets can make that would be unmistakable, that would advance dramatically the cause of freedom and peace. General Secretary Gorbachev, if you seek peace, if you seek prosperity for the Soviet Union and Eastern Europe, if you seek liberalization: Come here to this gate! Mr. Gorbachev, open this gate! Mr. Gorbachev, tear down this wall![28]

The Soviet Union's answer came in December 1989 in a summit with US president George H. W. Bush when Soviet president Gorbachev declared an end to the Cold War.

On November 9, 1989, the East German government announced that its citizens could freely cross over the wall to visit West Germany. Over the next few weeks, large groups of people helped chip away at the wall, and the barrier was eventually destroyed in 1990. That same year, on October 3, East and West German reunification was concluded. The Cold War was finally over, and the world found itself in what President George H. W. Bush would declare a "New World Order."

Post–Cold War Ghanaian president Kufuor and I discussed how the fall of the Berlin Wall impacted Africa's political direction:

> The Berlin Wall fell as a historic symbol to declare to the world that the Cold War was over. Initially everybody thought the world was going to be unipolar, that is, the West or the United States was going to be. But just around then, too, the ICT [information and communication technology] revolution had showed up, and people could see whatever was happening around the world at the same time, all over the world. Countries, now described as emergent or the BRICS countries.

The BRICS that he is referring to here is an acronym for Brazil, Russia, India, China, and South Africa, which are all considered to be at a similar stage of advanced economic development. President Kufuor continued,

> They came on the scene; even great China has started courting capitalism within its communist ideology, to the extent that now it is even a net lender to the United States, if you can believe it. Brazil, for instance, with its huge landmass, also came by smart leadership and very inventive on the agricultural front and a powerful trader. Russia with abundant natural resources also freeing itself from the sterile communism also started showing. So all these people came on the scene, and Africa, on our part, with the collapse of apartheid around then, and we started gaining self-confidence. Africa changed its continental union from the "Organization of African Unity," which was more to do with the free-

The streets of Durban, South Africa, 2008. Screenshot from *African Independence*.

The fall of the Berlin Wall in 1989. Screenshot from *African Independence*.

dom fighting to liberate Africa, to the "African Union," which is now focusing on the economic and social development of the continent and serious cooperation creating markets.

The end of the Cold War coincided with the end of apartheid. The demise of the two systems represented a new era in world politics. The victory against apartheid was the last independence movement on the African continent. Nelson Mandela was seen as representing a new relationship between Africa and the world. Africa was no longer going to be gauged by loyalty to capitalism or socialism, because socialism was now collaborating with capitalism and the Cold War was no more. The future would find Africa coming to terms with having more than just flag independence. As the situation changed, the economic, political, and military importance of Africa for the future of the world became even clearer.

4

APRIL 1994 AND BEYOND

African Independence Today

The last decade of the twentieth century was ushered in by the fall of the Berlin Wall. The Cold War was finally over, and the world found itself in a new global order. At this point the careful reader may recognize that I am suggesting that African independence is more than an event; it is an idea, and as an idea it continues to symbolize a change in the relationship between Africa and the world.

This chapter looks at the status of African independence as the era of international politics shaped by World War II came to an end. New energies were released across the continent for both good and evil. Independence in Africa found a new symbol to represent its rise on the African continent as the former inmate, Nelson Mandela, won a Nobel Peace Prize and was elected president of the new South Africa without apartheid. The impact was transformative and felt from Ghana to Kenya and Algeria. This new air of political independence left no historical stone unturned. Many of the new African republics do not have an inclusive historical narrative, and old colonial divisions led to a fresh third wave of independence movements from Ethiopia to Morocco. These political earthquakes continue to shake the frozen maps of post-colonial Africa.

The old questions of poverty and ethnic tensions continue to haunt the continent. Diseases rage across the continent. Malaria, AIDS, and ebola hit Africa harder than anywhere else in the world. Problems in African infrastructure and weak public health policies in much of the continent continue to make the region susceptible to epidemics like AIDS and ebola.

Political turmoil also marked 1994. The ugly head of ethnic conflict gave way to deadly confrontations. Genocide engulfed Rwanda while the world slept, and consequentially Zaire was destabilized into the Democratic Republic of the Congo (DRC) as Africa's first post-colonial regional "world war" erupted.

THE POST-INDEPENDENCE MAP OF AFRICA

In the aftermath of World War II, the world witnessed the rise of US economic, political, and military hegemony and the simultaneous rise of politically independent African republics. The US alliance with Western Europe and Japan became the leadership of the "free and democratic world." The alliance was reflected not only in a number of reconstruction projects like the Marshall Plan but also by close economic cooperation, political stability, and domination of international institutions—from the UN Security Council to the international financial institutions. The Cold War was not like other wars. During the Cold War, there was no actual military confrontation in Europe or the United States. Both the United States and the Soviet Union supported decolonization in Asia and Africa, a necessary step given the fall of the old empires of France and Britain in World War II.

The decolonized states were to participate in the existing economic arrangements defined by the politics of the Cold War and the emergence of the so-called Bretton Woods institutions. In July 1944, as World War II raged to an end, 730 delegates from the forty-four Allied nations met at the Mount Washington Hotel in Bretton Woods, New Hampshire, for the United Nations Monetary and Financial Conference to establish a new international monetary and financial order. At the meeting, the attendees established a system of rules, institutions, and procedures to regulate international monetary systems. It was here that the International Monetary Fund (IMF) and the International Bank for Reconstruction and Development (IBRD), which became part of the World Bank Group and focuses on making loans to so-called developing nations, were founded. These organizations and economic systems all took effect around the end of World War II.

The post-war period was marked by the international consolidation of military, political, and economic systems at the international level. The newly independent nations did not sit at the table while these reconfigurations were hammered out, but they were bound by the terms of the "New World Order." This explains in part why, in contrast, the first wave of independence was typically bloodless due to the willingness of colonizing nations to give up political power while retaining monopolies over the economic and military affairs of the new republics. There were exceptions to this, of course. For example, violent armed struggles occurred during the first wave of independence in Algeria and Kenya.

However, the second wave (approximately post-1970) was marked by protracted armed struggles and bloodshed in what we now know as Zimbabwe, Namibia, Angola, Mozambique, Guinea-Bissau, Cape Verde. South Africa was the last colony to gain political independence from the remains of classical European colonialism. However, it overlapped with the rise of a new movement for independence within the newly independent African states, namely, Namibia and Eritrea. The role played by Cuba in these struggles proved to be decisive in several cases, especially Angola and South Africa.

The third wave has been marked by new African republics born out of existing independent African nations. Armed struggles have also been characteristic of this third wave. This wave of struggles has resulted in the independence of Eritrea from Ethiopia, Namibia from South Africa, and South Sudan from Sudan. Perhaps the last nation in this third phase of independence is reflected in the case of the Western Sahara, which is still under Moroccan occupation. This third wave is distinguished from the other independence waves by the fact that the conflicts are within newly independent African nations.[1] Yet, like the previous independence movements against classical European colonialism, the more recent movement is changing the political map of Africa. These struggles completed the re-drawing of the map of post-independence Africa.

These third-wave independence movements are important and reflect the inability of African nations to consolidate the borders established by the colonial powers. They occurred after the independence of South Africa, which marks the end of the legacy of European classical colonialism on the African continent. I want to avoid presenting African independence as a failed cure for all the evils and problems that Africa has faced in the past, and which it continues to experience today. African independence marks the end of classical European colonialism, and this is an achievement. What happens after independence has as much to do with African agency as it does with the new post-war political, military, and economic reorganization of the world by the victor nations.

In this vein, it is instructive to consider the significance of South African political independence in order to gain an understanding of the promise and failures of post-independent African nations.

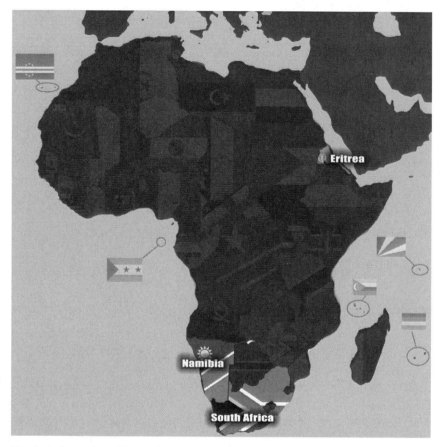

Newly Independent African States, 1995

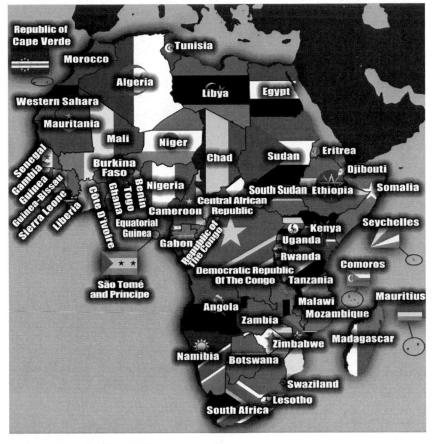

Political Map of Africa, 2015

APRIL 1994

The path to African political independence in South Africa was long and twisted. For many people, the life of Nelson Mandela has come to symbolize their struggle for freedom, justice, and equality. I remember watching the television footage of Mandela walking out of prison on February 11, 1990. After serving twenty-seven years, eighteen of them at the notorious Robben Island prison off the coast of Cape Town, Mandela was released from Victor Verster prison, and after a short ride to Cape Town, he addressed a huge crowd of supporters. He ended his remarks with the following words:

> Our march to freedom is irreversible. We must not allow fear to stand in our way. Universal suffrage on a common voters' role [sic] in a united democratic and non-racial South Africa is the only way to peace and racial harmony.
>
> In conclusion I wish to quote my own words during my trial in 1964. They are true today as they were then:
>
> > "I have fought against white domination and I have fought against black domination.
> >
> > I have cherished the ideal of a democratic and free society in which all persons live together in harmony and with equal opportunities.
> >
> > It is an ideal which I hope to live for and to achieve. But if needs be, it is an ideal for which I am prepared to die."[2]

In many of the new African republics, political constraints created by negotiated settlements curtailed the extent to which truth and justice could be pursued, which resulted in challenges to the legitimacy of the state. The political independence of Africans in South Africa serves as a testament to this process. And, while political independence is essential for the civic and human rights of the African population, the economic dynamics of the society continue to be marred by the persistence of racial inequality.

On December 10, 1993, news footage from around the world shows Nelson Mandela and F. W. de Klerk jointly receiving the Nobel Peace Prize. These two men in South Africa would come to symbolize the changes wrought by African independence more than any others on the continent. Mandela and de Klerk represented two different sides of the struggle for African rights and political independence. De Klerk represented the party that introduced apartheid and the Afrikaner people, so his efforts to transform South Africa into a non-apartheid state are worthy of consideration.

Nelson Mandela was the international symbol of the fight against apartheid. This system of racial segregation was the final and longest-lasting vestige of colonial domination in Africa. De Klerk won the Nobel Prize because it was his reforms that led to the end of apartheid. Mandela won the Nobel Prize because it was his form of struggle, strength, and integrity that led to the end of apartheid.[3]

The African independence movement was fought in the name of freedom, justice, and equality. The leadership of the movement saw themselves as the champions of democracy, and as a result they were often anti-capitalist. It was this anti-capitalism that got both Nkrumah and Lumumba in trouble during the movement for African independence. Most of these efforts to bring more democracy to the continent of Africa were not successful because of the colonial legacy of ethnic, racial, and religious conflict. In April 1994, African independence had a symbol to represent its new rise on the African continent as the former inmate, Mandela, began the next journey in his transformative politics.

April 1994 is one of the most momentous months in the history of African independence. While many writers cite May 31, 1910, as the date of South Africa's independence from Britain, Freedom Day is celebrated on April 27. The first democratic general elections in modern South African history took place on April 27, 1994. Millions queued in lines during the four-day voting period. Many Africans were voting for the first time. When the votes were counted, 62 percent went to the African National Congress. And, with great historical significance, the first act of the new National Assembly was to elect Nelson Rolihlahla Mandela the first democratically elected head of state.

Unlike the people of the nearly forty nations who were liberated during the first wave of the African independence movement, South Africa remained under the dominion of their colonial settlers until the end of the twentieth century, when the Afrikaner-controlled parliament finally agreed to hold South Africa's first free democratic elections. The muted voices of millions of South Africans were finally heard when they elected Mandela's African National Congress to power.[4]

The dreams of Africans in South Africa were centuries in the making. But more than just timing, the South African story has some essential differences from what occurred elsewhere in Africa. The Cold War was over, and liberated Africans thought they could choose what kind of freedom they wanted. In the case of South Africa, the former rulers were not going to leave the country. In the decades before 1994, many native South Africans lived in exile, traveling around the continent and the world. They witnessed the African independence movement firsthand and examined its successes along with its failures. When their opportunity came in 1994, Africans in South Africa awoke from their oppression armed with years of planning and preparation.

After taking control of a government that had for centuries been in the hands of their Afrikaner oppressors, Africans in South Africa could easily have used their new political power to exact revenge. But instead they instituted a policy of "non-racialism" and "reconciliation."[5] This was a necessary risk that may have laid the basis for the current questions around the ANC in South Africa following Mandela's presidency.

World attention toward Africa has for many years been driven more by disasters, famines, wars, and conflicts than the promise of Africa's many success stories. Over recent years, people outside of Africa sang "We are the World" and organized Band Aid, Live Aid, and Live 8, where politicians and celebrities demanded more responsible aid. However, with the last victory for the African independence movement in South Africa, people's views are starting to change because of Africa's strong decade of economic growth. The Africa rising story has begun to change the narrative for the better.

In September 1998, during a visit to the White House, President Nelson Mandela had this to say about President Bill Clinton's speech to the South African parliament earlier that year:

> When he addressed our Parliament, he almost brought down the walls of that building when he said, "We, in the United States, have been asking the wrong question. We have been saying, what can we do for Africa? That was the wrong question. The right question was, what can we do with Africa?"[6]

With the last independence struggle won, a new post–Cold War political reality came into view. However, time will tell if President Mandela's optimism was warranted.

POST-INDEPENDENCE UNITY

The new political map of Africa is not a map of one country. The political map of Africa contains over fifty-four different nations. In this age of regional organizations like the European Union, political unity among African nations remains a tricky issue as many of them have yet to consolidate

First post-apartheid South African president Nelson Mandela at the White House with President Bill Clinton and others in 1998. Screenshot from *African Independence*.

their national unity. However, in the post-1994 world, as evidenced by Mandela's words, hope is slowly returning to many African leaders.

Many Africans hoped that South Africa's political freedom represented an example of better days to come across the continent, but it was not going to be that simple. Just before South African independence, on April 7 of the same year, Rwanda's nightmare began. Almost one million people, mostly from the population called the Tutsi, a minority, were massacred during an extreme case of ethnic conflict.

Genocide engulfed Rwanda while the world seemed to ignore the disaster. Zaire continued to be consumed by internal strife, culminating in the overthrow of its longtime dictator Mobutu. New leadership renamed the country the Democratic Republic of the Congo. And Somalia remained a society with a weak bureaucratic authority. Political earthquakes were changing the situation of post–World War II Africa, and new methods of political resolution were changing the way conflict and crises were handled.[7]

The need for legitimacy in the new African republics led to states founded upon claims of traditions that justified the new nation and the constitutional democratic institutions—the bureaucracy. The traditional justification of the new African nations was founded upon the blood of the race, ethnic group, or religion. This was not new, nor is it isolated to Africa, as this approach serves as the basis of most modern states in the world. All nations have a story of the past that justifies the present existence of the state. Even the United States of America, a nation composed mainly of the descendants of immigrants (voluntary and involuntary), not to mention the indigenous populations, has a story about the founding fathers of Anglo-Saxon origins and the US Constitution as the basis of unity. The main strength of constitutions is their division of powers between branches of government and their other bureaucratic structures that defend individual and human rights. A crisis unfolds when the different branches of government do not work, or when the bureaucratic structures stop working in the defense of individual and human rights. This is referred to as corruption.

Bureaucratic legitimacy exists within a political context in which leaders of the state rhetorically advance the ideas of difference and nationalism. The Zulu, Ashanti, Kikuyu, Wolof, and thousands of other ethnic groups had an identity before colonialism and the arrival of Europeans. However, these identities were transformed under colonialism. As Africans were transformed into subjects of colonial rule, their identities were also transformed. Leaders of the African independence movement inherited their ideas of difference, nationalism, and citizenship from the colonial rulers. Indeed, unless the people were politically educated to think about their identity differently, as in states like Ghana and Tanzania, ethnic tensions remained a political factor.

The freedom fighters claimed to be more democratic and to foster more protections, on paper, for human and individual rights than the old colonial state. The new republics faced some of the same problems of legitimacy confronted by the colonial authorities. The transition of the former colony into a non-racial state would involve the use of traditional and bureaucratic claims of legitimacy. Each nation would have to create a national identity and develop the bureaucratic authority to run the new state. Such a transition requires that the truth be told about the hegemonic distortions of the racial state, and it requires the reconciliation of a tradition of unity into a vision of the future that respects the human and individual rights of all citizens while never forgetting the past. This was the struggle waged by the liberation movements across the continent: to change the structure of legitimacy in Africa and to ensure majority rule. They wanted Africans to accept the responsibility of government, to listen to an alternative narrative of the past, and to embrace a different tradition of citizenship. This transition from subject to citizen required a new vision, and this new vision required a change in the "mind-set" of the peoples of Africa.[8]

More than fifty independent African nations were born after four decades of struggle. As the drive for freedom and self-rule accelerated, Africa entered a golden age where everything seemed possible. Africans were independent, and equality was within sight. African independence was established politically, and new flags were added to the United Nations. However, flag independence did not necessarily result in a national identity or economic development. After fifty years of independence, national unity remains a problem for many important African nations. In fact, the problem of African unity on the continental level may be hampered by the lack of agreement as to the meaning of national unity, diversity of opinion, and the persistence of ethnic and religious conflicts.

TRADITIONAL ETHNIC CONFLICT

The African independence movements were nationalist. In almost all countries, people from all ethnic and religious backgrounds joined hands to topple colonial governments. However, despite the unity of purpose displayed at the national level, ethnic harmony in Africa has often been dysfunctional. During the time of colonial rule, European administrators used people's ethnic identities to govern. A few groups were favored and co-opted by colonial governments while others were marginalized and excluded from both the political and economic processes of the colonies.

During the period of African independence, many of these different ethnic groups were organized to support the movement. Ethnicity in Africa was good in that it allowed a person to identify with a larger nation and was used as the basis for African nationalism. Colonial governments could implement their policy of divide and rule because across the continent, ethnic groups have tended to be exclusive in their membership, and thus they tend to support nepotism and corruption. During colonial rule, this was the objective. While this was not the object of the independence movement, in the case of political competitions, elections, and so forth, ethnic identity is often the main weapon in national politics.[9]

The new African flags symbolized the success of the African independence movements. Under colonial authority, ethnicity and tribe were described as synonymous and were presented as groups that are culturally identifiable through language, religion, or some particular cultural or social practice. Difference, including ethnic and religious groups, may have existed before the arrival of colonial rule in Africa, but, under colonial rule, ethnicity was used as an important identifier.

Rwanda is a perfect example of the catastrophic potential of traditions of ethnic conflict. In order to understand just how catastrophic requires looking at the present with an eye to the past. Ethnic identity in Rwanda had its roots in colonial governance. On April 7, 2014, twenty years after the genocide in Rwanda, President Paul Kagame had this to say as he reflected on the roots of his nation's genocidal past in a *Wall Street Journal* op-ed:

> The most devastating legacy of European control of Rwanda was the transformation of social distinctions into "races." We were classified and dissected, and whatever differences existed were magnified according to a framework invented elsewhere. Rwanda's two thousand years of history were reduced to a series of caricatures based on Bible passages and on myths told to credulous explorers.

By the time Belgium gained full control of the then Rwanda-Urundi colony in 1923, Tutsis and Hutus had been living in relative harmony for ages. But in order to establish their control, Belgium established a policy of identity cards, dividing the population between Tutsis and Hutus. In this way, they were able to distinguish the Tutsis—who would soon be a minority ruling class in their colony—from the Hutus. After independence and ensuing decades of ethnic clashes, the Hutu majority population gained control of the government. By the early 1990s, hundreds of thousands of Tutsis lived in exile in neighboring countries. These conflicts led to a civil war between the government of President Juvénal Habyarimana and the rebel Rwanda Patriotic Army (RPA), the armed wing of the Rwanda Patriotic Front (RPF). In the 1990s, the civil war heated up with several intense battles, which ultimately led to a stalemate followed by peace negotiations and the signing of the Arusha Accords in 1993. This agreement would have led to a power-sharing government. It was within this colonially created situation that the dry tinder of the later genocidal fires began to smolder.[10]

On the morning of April 7, 1994, the people living in the lush rolling hills outside of Kigali, Rwanda, awoke to discover that their Hutu president Habyarimana, and the Burundian president Cyprien Ntaryamira, had been assassinated as they returned from a peace summit in Tanzania. A missile had shot down their plane. In the midst of a civil war, the Hutu government seized the news to foment a counterattack on the advancing

Tutsi rebels. But instead of attacking soldiers, Hutu militias set their sights on unarmed Tutsi civilians. Over the next three months, ethnic cleansing would erupt across the countryside as Hutus brutally began attacking and killing defenseless Tutsis in order to avenge the death of their president. Armed with crude machetes, Hutu militias slaughtered over eight hundred thousand Tutsi civilians in a mere three months, marking this as one of the worst cases of genocide, comparable to the Nazi Holocaust of World War II.[11] A significant number of moderate Hutus who opposed the mass slaughter of Tutsis were also targeted and killed.

President Kagame returned to Rwanda from Uganda, even as the world turned away in horror at the genocide. He and his Tutsi-based Rwanda Patriotic Front eventually won Rwanda's civil war, took control of the Rwandan government, and have transformed Rwanda into one of the most stable and economically prosperous countries in Africa during the first years of the twenty-first century.

Like in Rwanda, Kenya provides another excellent example of the problem of ethnic conflict. Between 1952 and 1960, during the Kenyan people's struggle for independence, the British detained, brutalized, and murdered hundreds of thousands of people. This state of emergency ended in 1960, and in 1963 Kenya became independent, with Jomo Kenyatta as its president. His presidency is controversial, some believing he started a culture of corruption by giving the best pieces of land to his family and friends from his ethnic group. On the other hand, Kenya became part of the United Nations and reached its goal of military stability, even if the nation continued to be plagued by poverty.

Kenya has over seventy different ethnic groups, with the five largest consisting of the Kikuyu, Luhya, Luo, Kalenjin, and Kamba. Beginning with the first post-independence government of Jomo Kenyatta and extending up to the twenty-first century, Kenya's elections have been dominated by strong ethnic identification and regionalism.

In the heart of downtown Nairobi stands a beautiful memorial commemorating Jomo Kenyatta, who ruled Kenya until he died in August 1978. After Kenyatta's passing, Vice President Daniel arap Moi became acting president and was reelected several times over the next two decades, a period in which Kenya held its first multi-party elections. In 2002, the presidency of Moi came to an end when Mwai Kibaki was elected Kenya's third president. The political terrain was complicated by the rise of a popular opposition led by Raila Amolo Odinga, the son of Jaramogi Oginga Odinga, the opposition leader under Jomo Kenyatta. The 2007 election would be between Kibaki and Raila Odinga. The disputed contest between the two former political allies intensified Kenya's ethnic conflict between December 2007 and February 2008.

The two main coalitions seeking political power in the 2007 elections were the Orange Democratic Movement (ODM) led by Odinga and the Party of National Unity (PNU) led by Kibaki. Both coalitions became focused on ethnically oriented political constituencies. The PNU was the party of the Kikuyu based in the Central Province, communities in the Eastern Province with large groups in Nairobi, and the Rift Valley. The ODM was the party of the Nairobi slums; the Luo, Luhya, and Kalenjin from the coast; Nyanza and Western provinces; and the Rift Valley.

After the voting, Kibaki was declared the winner and was immediately sworn in as president. The ODM rejected the results, as did the European Union elections monitors. There was widespread violence as a result of the elections. More than one thousand people were killed, and nearly seven hundred thousand were internally displaced from their homes. The violence was finally stopped when several eminent African politicians negotiated a power-sharing deal that was accepted by both parties. In the compromise, Odinga became prime minister, and Kibaki continued as president.

After the power-sharing agreement had been concluded and he was comfortably in office, I asked Prime Minister Odinga if he still believed that the election was rigged. "Not even a fool would doubt that in this country," he replied.

Interview with Raila Odinga, prime minister of the Republic of Kenya (2008 and 2013), in Nairobi, Kenya, 2008. Screenshot from *African Independence*.

Investigations by the International Criminal Court (ICC) led to recommendations that several Kenyan politicians be put on trial for crimes against humanity. Among the individuals charged by the ICC was Uhuru Kenyatta, the son of former president Jomo Kenyatta. In 2013, he was elected president after an intense campaign against Prime Minister Raila Odinga. Kenyatta's election is seen by many as a rejection of the ICC processes by the people of Kenya.[12] Such rejection may be a legitimate response to what seems like an African focus of the ICC; however, the national context of many African politicians has fostered ethnic conflict.

Prime Minister Odinga offers some insight about these issues in Kenya after independence from Britain.

> I want to say that we made quite a tremendous progress so far. The struggle to democratize this country is as old as this country has been independent. There have been two forces, pulling in two opposite directions: the forces for the retention of the status quo versus the forces for democracy. In other words, at independence, there were two groups: those who wanted to inherit the privileged positions of the British and use it to lord it over their fellow Kenyans, and those who wanted to see greater participation of the people of this country, the governors. So this struggle has taken different turns at different times. Sometimes it has been peaceful. Sometimes it has been violent. It has been progressive and consistent. So, where we are, you can see accumulation of the efforts that have been made by people at different times in our country's history.
>
> History of ethnicity or tribalism is colonialism. Kenyatta, when he was challenged ideologically by my father, receded into his ethnic cocoon, in order to fight for his survival. Then after Kenyatta surrounded himself fast with an elite from his community, to the exclusion of others. After him, Moi came in, and Moi said he was following in the footsteps of Kenyatta. So he fired most of the Kenyatta cronies and brought in his own from his community.
>
> So what I am saying is that this has influenced our politics. Since the advent of the multi-partyism, ethnicity has always been a factor in the elections. Next door, Mwalimu Julius Nyerere, in spite of the weaknesses of some of his policies or failures, he was able at least to forge one united nation called Tanzania. Tanzanians don't have these hang-ups or hangovers, about this is the person coming from this or this tribe, for they never asked. So by creating greater unity and values to which people can aspire, you can actually make ethnicity irrelevant. This is what we want to do in this country.

In neighboring Zaire, as Mobutu fled the country, the Alliance des Forces Démocratiques pour la Libération du Congo-Zaïre (AFDL) drove the regular Zairean army out of the country and declared the Democratic Republic of the Congo in 1997. The AFDL was the coalition that brought Laurent Kabila to power. After successfully overthrowing the Mobutu dictatorship, the alliance of dissidents fell apart within the country, as did Kabila's regional alliance with Uganda and Rwanda, plunging the country back into civil conflict and a weak government. With the support of Angola, Namibia, and Zimbabwe, Laurent Kabila's son Joseph was installed into power. However, the country remains embroiled in conflict, particularly in eastern Congo.[13]

Across much of Africa, ethnic differences have been exploited by the ruling elite to keep itself in power through hatred and fear of other social groups. Many a time, these actions have pushed the boundaries of ethnic identity to the extremes, resulting in ethnic conflict over political and economic power and control of land as witnessed at the beginning of the twenty-first century. So intense is ethnic conflict that it can turn into political and military conflict over the legitimacy of the state. Movements for independence within the new republics erupted in Eritrea and South Sudan, and civil conflicts and war are ever present in nations as far apart as Nigeria, the Central African Republic, Sierra Leone, Côte d'Ivoire, Liberia, Algeria, Libya, and Egypt.

Ethnic and religious conflict continues as a major concern in the African republics. The story of elections in Kenya, genocide in Rwanda, political destabilization in the DRC, civil war and ethnic conflict in the Sudan, the Boko Haram in Nigeria, and other conflicts elsewhere attest to the difficulties in establishing traditional legitimacy of the new republics and how this reality is interpreted in international arenas.[14] Ethnic and religious differences continue to be used as weapons against Africa and will do so until unity becomes a priority.

African republics must do more to create a narrative that supports the legitimacy of the new state above ethnic identity. In the absence of such changes, they are vulnerable to internal and external forces that use ethnicity and religion as weapons of disorganization. Until the people embrace a history of a common identity as well as broad-based social, economic, and political inclusion, the threat of ethnic and religious conflict will remain a problem and a threat to peace and stability. Odinga's comment about the absence of ethnic conflict in Tanzania is most important in understanding how there is hope for solving this seemingly intractable problem.

Africa must reconcile its past of colonial manipulations and ethnic conflict in order to have a brighter future. The colonial state used and created ethnic and religious identities as a weapon against the unity of African communities. Reconciliation requires building a democratic future and a functioning bureaucracy anchored on good governance and inclusive, equitable, and sustainable development.

For these new republics, the intersection of old traditions, new constitutions, human and individual rights, and truth and reconciliation commissions are essential. The examples of South Africa and Rwanda show that solutions can be found. They may not serve all interests or solve every problem, but they help create a space for people to get their lives back on track. The past authoritarian rules of the colonial powers required reformulating ideas about citizenship in a context of justice, freedom, and new equalities, even if these documents were only words yet to be realized within the new republics.

HYPOCRISY, TERROR, AID, AND CRIME

The United States first declared war against terrorism in the 1980s during the Regan presidency. Libya was involved in an attack on American soldiers in the 1986 West Berlin nightclub bombing. By April, Reagan declared war against international terrorism, sending American bombers against Libya. The new war is against "terror." The use of the word "terror" is itself debatable and subject to many different interpretations and misuses. However, all definitions consider premeditated, politically motivated violence perpetrated against non-combatant targets by groups or individuals as essential components. In reality, this kind of definition is only as strong as the person making the argument. That is, the argument depends on the idea of terrorism as an act against the legitimate institutions in a society or the "international community." Those with power engage in the premeditated and politically motivated violence perpetrated against non-combatants on a normal basis in war. The monopoly on the use of violence is what is in question here, and this is the basis of the hypocrisy.

So, state-sponsored terror is the biggest offender. The independence movements in Asia and Africa accused colonial governments of organized violence against the colonized citizens. Anti-racism movements continue to make claims of governmental premeditated violence against ethnic, religious, and racially marginalized citizens in North America and, more recently, in Latin America and other areas of the world. Many of the so-called terrorist groups that even take credit for terrorist acts justify their violence on the basis of state violence perpetuated by the United States and Europe against the formerly colonized areas of Asia and Africa.

The international fight against violence today is not non-violence, as was the hope of Mahatma Gandhi and Martin Luther King Jr. Nor is the fight against violent state power holders easily changed using non-violent tactics. No, the fight against violence today is discussed in the language of the gun used by Hitler and Churchill. The political motivation for engaging violence with violence is "terror." And the current war around the world is with terror. However, this definition of terror as violence against the innocent leads to the uncomfortable reality of the modern hypocrisy of international affairs. If it is a crime of terror for a government or even a clandestine agent to kill people for unjustifiable reasons, it is wrong for the United States and its allies to kill innocent people or to arm people that will kill innocent people in the name of fighting this same terror.

The use of violence is a question of perspective. Nelson Mandela challenged George H. W. Bush on his call for all parties in the war around apartheid to "renounce the use of violence and armed struggle." This shows how one's point of view is very important. Mandela answered Bush's challenge by declaring that the racially structured apartheid government's use of violence against black people was the reason that "the people have no alternative but to resort to violence." President Bush would not have argued against the need for violence in the American Revolutionary War, but he seemed not to see the same urgency in South Africa. The war against terrorism has had a profound impact on other parts of Africa as well. Africa is full of examples of this current fight. And what is called "terror" is used as a justification for most civil and international conflicts.

For example, more than two years before the September 11, 2001, attack on the twin towers in New York City and the Pentagon, the war on terror was being fought like the Cold War, and Africa was once again in the middle. A clear example of Africa's involvement is the attacks on the US embassies in Dar es Salaam and Nairobi on August 7, 1998. Trucks laden with explosives simultaneously attacked both US embassies. Combined, the attacks resulted in over two hundred deaths and five thousand injuries. World news organizations broadcasted images of the carnage in the aftermath at the Nairobi embassy. The explosives were directed at American institutions, but most of the victims were from Kenya and Tanzania. The news reports that followed made al-Qaeda and Osama bin Laden known to the world.[15]

In Nairobi, the embassy was transformed into a body-strewn battlefield. Rescue workers carried bodies after the bombings. One photo broadcasted around the world shows rescue workers in Kenya carrying the body of a woman over the rubble of a building destroyed by the terrorist bombing. I asked a survivor of the Nairobi bombings, Naomi Kerongo, for a firsthand account of what happened in Kenya.

> Yes, I was in my office, on tenth floor of the Cooperative House where I served the government of Kenya as a trade development officer in the Ministry of Commerce and Industry. Then, after the bombing, when the blast went on, I came to watch at the window which faces the railways, to see outside if it is an accident or a carjacker who has been shot or something. There was a smaller blast. Then I saw somebody laying down inside here somewhere. I said maybe a carjacker has been shot dead. Then the big blast came and shook the building, you know. It was uprooted, shaken, and planted back. And, that is when I, I think I, I cannot account how or what happened. I think I died.
>
> A glass went here, and this was going too deep. And now I lost my memory, I lost consciousness, and for two years I was in hospital.

Naomi's suffering occurs within a very changed international political system. And the fight against terror has produced a response to the East African terror attacks that reflect a continuation of past policies that ignore African realities in order to consider international strategic issues. The post–Cold War world is different. The Soviet Union is gone. The only remaining global world power is the United States. While challenges from China, India, Russia, and Brazil are important, the West under the leadership of the United States continues to be an important player on the African continent.

On September 11, 2001, when the attack on New York happened, I turned on my television. The first thing I saw on the news coverage was the smoke and flames coming from the World Trade Center towers where the first and then the second plane had crashed. The broadcasters were discussing reports that a plane cruising at abnormally low altitudes had crashed into the World Trade Center tower. In 2001, the war on terrorism was restated in response to the World Trade Center attack on the United States. And the war was accelerated in Afghanistan, Iraq, and several nations in Africa (including Somalia, Kenya, Mali, Libya, Algeria, Egypt, South Africa, and the Sudan).

Terrorism in Africa cannot be separated from its international and regional context. It is important to understand how al-Qaeda and related organizations figure into the context of Africa. World attention is turning to the rise of so-called Islamic movements across Africa with the al-Shabaab movement in Somalia, Boko Haram in Nigeria, and Islamic Maghred (AQIM) and Ansar Dine in the north. Terrorism has become a major threat on the African continent. How the United States and international coalitions against terrorism respond to the peoples in Africa and Asia is as important as attacks of terror that occur in the United States and Europe. All people's lives matter, and they require that we respect how any fight for justice is carried out. We are all only as good as our actions.

In April 2010, the world was shocked when the whistle-blowing website WikiLeaks published a classified video called *Collateral Murder*. Shot from an Apache helicopter on patrol in the Iraqi suburb of New Baghdad in July 2007, the video shows two Apache helicopters killing eleven people, including two Reuters news employees (photojournalist Namir Noor-Eldeen and his driver Saeed Chmagh), and wounding two children. The soldiers request and are granted permission to open fire, and while the video is a compelling testament to the harm being done, the audio presents the soldiers joking about the dead and dying civilians under their 30 mm cannon fire. The army investigation into the attack ultimately found that the helicopter crew had followed the "rules of engagement." The International Criminal Court did nothing in the case, and in fact could not have done anything because the United States was not a signatory to the ICC.

The establishment of the United States African Command (AFRICOM) is solely dedicated to US security interests in Africa. In recent years, AFRICOM has been expanding its operations on the African continent. In his speech to West Point graduates on May 24, 2014, President Barack Obama outlined this shift in US military strategy. The new strategy is based on what is seen as the successes of the US military presence in Afghanistan. Obama argued,

> Together with our allies, America struck huge blows against al Qaeda core and pushed back against an insurgency that threatened to overrun the country. But sustaining this progress depends on the ability of Afghans to do the job. And that's why we trained hundreds of thousands of Afghan soldiers and police. Earlier this spring, those forces, those Afghan forces, secured an election in which Afghans voted for the first democratic transfer of power in their history. And at the end of this year, a new Afghan President will be in office and America's combat mission will be over.
>
> Now, that was an enormous achievement made because of America's armed forces. But as we move to a train-and-advise mission in Afghanistan, our reduced presence allows us to more effectively address emerging threats in the Middle East and North Africa. So, earlier this year, I asked my national security team to develop a plan for a network of partnerships from South Asia to the Sahel.[16]

In this new strategy, the United States would not need a major presence on the ground. Instead, a regionalized strategy of supporting partners has emerged. These new partnerships reflect what the United States means by "work with Africa."[17] The new partnerships are reflected in efforts such as supporting the multi-national forces in Somalia, training security and border patrols in Libya, and facilitating French operations in northern Mali. When necessary, these efforts would be complemented by direct action on the ground and in the air with airstrikes, including drone strikes—or, as in the words of Obama, "through capture operations like the one that brought a terrorist involved in the plot to bomb our embassies in 1998 to face justice." Unlike China, the US policy in Africa continues to prioritize military and security issues, while economic considerations remain secondary.

Some African leaders like President Mkapa consider much of the fight against terrorism as cover for politically motivated actions. In his reference to what became known as the Arab Spring, mass protest and military coups, which mainly took place in North Africa, President Mkapa's comments are quite definitive. What many saw as the battle for more democracy, he sees as a cover for political and economic interests. He told me,

> I see the North African episode as really an effort to get rid of countries, of regimes that were, that were trying to assert their independence and their sovereignty over their resources. There is a democratic tinge to it, but the predominant factor for their fall was the determination of the NATO countries to continue their dominance over the resources of Northern Africa.

Economic dominance has continued to prevent the recognition of the democratic aims of the people of Africa. Aid comes to Africa in many forms, but rarely does it result in meeting the democratic needs of the people of Africa. Increasingly, aid in Africa comes as a result of the strategic interests of the European nations, the United States, and China. Military aid may be the largest single category, but the other types of aid receive much more attention in US and Western international media. I asked President Benjamin Mkapa what he thought about the external forces such as the United Nations, the International Criminal Court, the International Monetary Fund, and the World Bank, and their impact on Africa today. This is what he had to say:

> Seriously speaking, we should now see the necessity, the unavoidable imperative, of establishing a new world order. The old world order was devised by the so-called victor nations of the Second World War. When the IMF was formed, the World Bank was formed, when all these other

international organizations were formed, we were either young states or non-existent states. But now we are states, and there are as many as fifty-three of us now on the African continent. We were not there when these charters were being drawn. We were not there when we were describing the kind of international relations values which are espoused by these organizations, and you see the result is that now because of our independence, and because of the BRICS, for instance, the new emerging countries, and the limited natural resources there are in this world, which are necessary for development, there is rivalry. There is rivalry between them. It is not a war, but there is rivalry. How can you say that the UN can continue to have only five members of the Security Council? How can that possibly be? How can you say sovereignty over natural resources can only be defined by the principles declared by the victor powers in the Second World War? No, that is untenable. Otherwise they'll be the source of friction, they'll be a source of violence, and perhaps it will be a source of war.

President Mkapa is not alone in his critique of the current role of international organizations in Africa. For example, the International Criminal Court has been accused of being anti-African. The ICC was established in 2002 to prosecute claims of genocide, crimes against humanity, and war crimes. Many human rights groups had hoped the court would help end what many see as impunity in world political leadership, especially in African politics. Africa needs assistance in administering justice, especially among the powerful and violent.

African nations make up almost a third of the states that have signed and ratified the ICC's Rome Statute. As of 2013, several important states have not signed the statute, including the United States, China, Japan, India, Israel, and Turkey. As of 2013, the ICC had eight open investigations, and all eight were in Africa. Given the over-representation of Africans before the court, the appearance of wrongdoing is obvious to many observers.

In 2014, the presidents of Sudan and Kenya faced charges for crimes against humanity. The prosecution of Kenya's leadership for crimes against humanity stems from the riots associated with the 2008 presidential election, and the outstanding warrant of arrest for Sudan's Omar al-Bashir for war crimes in Darfur.[18] Similarly, the people in the Sudan did not appear to simply support the ICC case against al-Bashir. The election of Kenyatta in Kenya and the rallies in support of al-Bashir against the ICC case represent a kind of popular opinion.

Kenyatta's attendance at the hearings marked a historic moment for transparency in Africa. A sitting head of state took leave of his office and went to the International Criminal Court hearings around the ethnic violence associated with the 2008 presidential election. Kenyatta became the first sitting head of state to appear before the ICC. Kenyatta was absolved of wrongdoing.

In fact, the Sudanese and Kenyan responses represent African popular response to the ICC's unequal focus on African leadership. We should be careful in the interpretation of the popular rejection of the ICC decisions as support for the individual leaders; however, these facts, and the political and structural inequalities mentioned by President Mkapa, attest to the need for a change in the relationship between Africa and the world.

The world and Africa would greatly benefit from an International Criminal Court that is not so clearly lacking in the appearance of being fair, competent, and independent. The ICC was established in 2002 among much fanfare that it would be able to effectively help Africa and the world. African states overwhelmingly supported the creation of the court in hopes that it would help assure that those perpetrating atrocities would no longer escape paying for their crimes against the people. A fair court would pursue all serious international crimes within its mandate, wherever they occur in the world, and would not target particular regions. In part, the United States and Israel have refused to accede to the ICC because they see the court as subject to political manipulation. One might ask if the court would have the resources or political will to pursue the claims from those at war with the United States and Israel.

The role of the major world economic and donor organizations are also being called into question. After the Cold War and the freedom of Nelson Mandela, the world witnessed a sea change in the role and relationships between some of the former Third World nations and the former colonial powers. This change resulted in a new debate that had an anti-Western aid side and pro-Western aid advocates.[19]

This debate has been transformed by the rise of the South, particularly that of China, Brazil, and India. With the rise of the BRICS (Brazil, Russia, India, China, and South Africa), new possibilities are surfacing about how the future could look. The reintegration of South Africa onto the international scene confirmed that Africa could have a place at this new table of economic configurations. In the post–Cold War period, the BRICS are not a superpower, and they are not at war with the only surviving superpower—the United States.

President Benjamin Mkapa had this to say:

> I would like to see it end as quickly as possible, foreign aid, because I think it has really, it has affected our attitude towards development. We are putting too much, too much hope and trust upon the power

of development assistance, as it is called. As a person, I don't like being a beggar. And secondly, as a country, I don't like my country being a beggar, but the way aid is presented to us is as if we are beggars, and beggars, and beggars, and that's wrong. But to think of development aid and assistance as the crux of the financial or capital inputs to our development is entirely wrong, and so I would like to urge that African states, I would urge them to try to distance themselves from the imperative of aid, to try to decouple themselves from the aid fixation. And that will really release their energies for development in dignity.

The world needs to work with Africa for development. This will enhance African dignity in the relationship with the world. The process of African unification may take years. However, progress in regional integration in areas such as trade and the free movement of people in some regional economic communities offers hope.

Post-independence Africa is marked by the imperative of reconciliation toward the future represented by South Africa's election of Nelson Mandela. However, recognition of Africa's place in the new world order has lagged behind the fight against terror, and the blind pursuit of national strategic interests has taken priority over a desperately needed emphasis on world strategic interests. This needed change in perspective has been recognized in terms of the environment. We all need individual nations to do their part in preserving the natural environment for human survival. Thus, there exists an international movement that supports African ecological preservation, some in honest collaboration with African-based individuals and institutions. However, the so-called war on terror and the witch hunt for African leaders by the ICC has increasingly become a substitute for meaningful action and dialogue about Africa's future.

The overemphasis on what aid can deliver and the lack of consideration of the strategic interests of the world have diminished the relevance of Africa in the United States and Europe. If the West wanted to take Africa seriously, then the African Union would have been granted a permanent place at the so-called G20 table. I know that the everyday person in the West is weary of the calls for more aid to Africa, especially after the 2008 global financial crisis. South Africa and other African countries are playing an important role in international relations on the world stage. A change is needed for those that publicly present their relationships with Africa in terms of humanitarian aid while in fact their main consideration is in maintaining the economic advantages they received following World War II and the Cold War. Ignoring Africa's real economic and demographic strengths is simply bad public policy and has led Europe and North America to lose their global influence and trade advantages, put in place by the Bretton Woods institutions, to the emerging BRICS in Asia, Africa, and South America.

Good and productive diplomatic and trade engagement with Africa on an equitable footing is essential. Not because of the goodness of people—this motivation has shown itself to be a cover for the selfish interests of maintaining antiquated polices in a new global world. This need to change should be motivated by doing the right thing and planning for a future that goes beyond inequalities created in the past.

EXTENDING AFRICAN INDEPENDENCE

It did not take long for the nascent African republics to falter as the Cold War and underdevelopment turned the dream of African independence into a nightmare. When the Cold War was over, Africans still had the ethnic and racial problems fostered by colonial rule. And today, Africa finds itself in a world of international development agencies, China's entrance onto the world scene as a major economic and political player, and the creation of the European Union. An important role in global economic and financial governance has been promoted by the development of groupings of economic blocs. The Group of Seven, known as the G7, was born in 1975 at Rambouillet under the French president Valéry d'Estaing and German chancellor Helmut Schmidt with heads of state and governments of the most advanced capitalist economies, including Canada, Italy, Japan, the United Kingdom, and the United States. In 1998, Russia joined what became the G8. In 1999, the G20 came into existence as a forum for cooperation between the most advanced industrial nations and the emerging-market countries to promote economic stability. The G20 held its first meeting under the chairmanship of Canadian finance minister Paul Martin. The G7, G8, and the G20 have begun to replace the political space of the old Bretton Woods institutions in the new world economic order. In all of these organizations, Africa has a small or insignificant role. Only South Africa is a member of the G20. Thus, once again, one of the wealthiest continents in the world has been placed in a secondary role on the international stage of economic planning.

Many African leaders think that Africa's quest for durable peace and development in this brave new world requires greater African unity and regional integration. Kwame Nkrumah had argued that Africa would not be liberated until it was unified into one nation. In a way, Nkrumah was arguing that African independence was only a step in the right direction.[20] In 1963, Nkrumah published *Africa Must Unite*, and in its pages he argued,

> For we have dedicated ourselves to the attainment of total African freedom. Here is one bond of unity that allies free Africa with unfree Africa, as well as all those independent states dedicated to this cause. My party, the Convention People's Party, fervently upholds, as an unquestionable right, the burning aspirations of the still subjected peoples of our continent for freedom. Since our inception, we have raised as a cardinal policy, the total emancipation of Africa from colonialism in all its forms. To this we have added the objective of the political union of African states as the securest safeguard of our hard-won freedom and the soundest foundation for our individual, no less than our common, economic, social and cultural advancement.[21]

I asked several African political leaders what they thought were the prospects of a United States of Africa. President Kaunda said,

> It's coming. Not during our time, I'm sure not. But definitely, whatever we do, we must contribute to the birth of the African Union. It's coming. Look at Europe. Two different world wars, 1914 to 1918, 1939 to 1945—two world wars. Today, Europe is coming together. They

In front of the African Union monument in Accra, Ghana, 2011. Jabari Zuberi/TZ Production Company.

have left the wars history behind. They are now fighting for the euro, to have like United States of America dollar; they want to have a euro in Europe. They have come together by using the euro, a number of them. So, Africa is not different.

President Mkapa added,

> The United States of Africa is a dream. We must work towards it. . . . We are realizing that development also will come with greater unity between these member states of the African Union. Because there are, there are certain levels of development which can only be attained regionally, conceived regionally. Resources mobilization for the realization has got to be regional, and implementation has got to be regional, with safeguards for every, every cooperant. You have the Economic Community of West African states, you have the Central African States Organization, we have the Southern African Development Community, we have the East African Community, and so, and so more and more we are embracing the imperative of cooperation and unity as a tool, as a weapon of our development. And, for the realization of real freedom in development, yes.

In a park named after her father, I asked Samia Nkrumah about the relevance of her father's definition of Pan-Africanism as the total liberation and unification of Africa under scientific socialism.

Interview with Benjamin Mkapa, third president of the United Republic of Tanzania, in Johannesburg, South Africa, 2012. Screenshot from *African Independence*.

Precisely that, because he was concerned with meeting our basic social needs. For many of us, the unification of the continent is inevitable if we want to become an economic force. We know that we cannot compete with the bigger blocs that exist today. So if we want to become economically strong, I think there's no other option, no other option, but to pool our resources and our energies together. There have been many since Kwame Nkrumah's proposal in '63, and attempts at, you know, promoting African unity.

And I think we will revisit it more and more as the years go by. I think many of us believe that this is the way forward.

While Africa has yet to be organized into a United States of Africa, many international policies are directed at the continent as if it is one geopolitical unit. This may be an indication of Africa's current place in the world.

I asked President Kenneth Kaunda to place this reality in context with the image that many people of Africa are afflicted by a lack of unity, poverty, war, and disease. He told me,

Those who think like that, young man, must remember, there was a slave trade. The slave trade, colonization of the continent. Now, to fight, start fighting from there—slave trade, colonization, apartheid—wasn't an easy thing. We have fought, we have fought, and thank the good Lord God almighty, we have won. We have won. Now we are fighting to build a fresh outward Africa. It is not easy, but we have started doing that.

In this new Africa, China has become a major economic and political actor. After World War II, China viewed its political interests as the same as the African people's fight for independence. Africa and China had both suffered at the hands of the imperialist powers under colonial rule. At the 1955 Bandung Conference, the largest meeting of Asian and African states took place. Several of the attending nations were newly independent republics. The official documents from the conference stated that its purpose was to promote African and Asian economic, cultural, and political cooperation in the fight for development and against colonialism and neo-colonialism. The efforts of the conference led to the Non-Aligned Movement. Beginning with the 1955 meeting, Zhou Enlai, the first premier of the People's Republic of China, led his nation's efforts to internally advance China's use of its foreign aid to Africa as an instrument to advance China's political interests. Over the years, China has provided significant amounts of foreign aid to Africa despite its own domestic poverty and underdevelopment.

With His Excellency Kenneth Kaunda, president of Zambia (1964–1991), after interview, 2010. Jabari Zuberi/TZ Production Company.

On the global level, China has assumed a leadership position and substantially increased its activities in Africa. And the new African republics have been a good friend to China's international political profile. The fifty-four African states account for more than a fourth of the UN member states, and many a time they have supported China's political agenda.[22]

I discussed the implications of China in Africa with two different African leaders and got two very different responses. President Kufuor had this to say:

> Well, it's an open world now. We talk of "global village." And China has taken the lead economically, doing serious business and is very competitive, but we are talking democracy and governance which goes beyond just economic performance and outreach, so what I am saying is that times are coming when the interactions and relationships will get more and more total and comprehensive, not just economic.

In his comments, President Kufuor implies, with good reason, that China does not use aid to dictate the policies of African countries. Chinese economic policies in Africa are at historically high levels. In 2012, China spent $3 billion in foreign direct investment in Africa, and China-Africa trade reached almost $200 billion. To place this in context, in the same year, Chinese trade with the European Union was $546 billion, and trade with the United States was $485 billion. I interpret Kufuor's comments to suggest that China is overemphasizing the economic benefits of trade with Africa and neglecting Africa's long-term political interests. In this way, China's policies are not very different from those of the West in the past and today.

President Mkapa, a critic of the idea of aid in general, had a very different reply as he discussed China's history and current aid programs:

> China is doing everything positive for Africa. I know the media in the West are painting this Chinese dragon that is about to consume us in Africa. Nothing could be further from truth. China was extremely instrumental, decisively instrumental, in support for the liberation struggles of Mozambique, of Zimbabwe, of Namibia, and so on. They were instrumental because they trained the freedom fighters, but they also helped with the arms for the freedom fighters, so that was their first positive contact with, with independent Africa. After these countries became independent, China has been a major, a major donor country, an aid donor. It helped us, for instance, to build the Tanzania–Zambia railway line when in our struggle to free Zambia from too much dependence on South African ports, because South Africa was then under, under apartheid. So, they have built very many other schemes in health, in education, and then of course in building the armed forces of several African countries. That is on the donor level, but as investors, now, you know, five decades after independence they are also a trading nation. I know the West is very suspicious of this, but that is because they really generally believe that we were their backyard. We in Africa we were their backyard, no. So the Chinese are proving them wrong.

President Mkapa seems to support the argument that China's interest is in helping Africa achieve development without meddling in the internal affairs of African countries through the Western policy of conditional aid. While this may be true, we must also recognize that Chinese aid to Africa increases access to Africa's natural resources and local markets, as well as support for Beijing's "one China" policy.

On his 2009 trip to Africa, US president Barack Obama told the Ghanaian people,

> I'm speaking to you at the end of a long trip. I began in Russia for a summit between two great powers. I traveled to Italy for a meeting of the world's leading economies. And I've come here to Ghana for a

His Excellency Benjamin Mkapa and other guests at the 2010 African Presidential Roundtable official dinner, 2010. Jabari Zuberi/TZ Production Company.

simple reason: The 21st century will be shaped by what happens not just in Rome or Moscow or Washington, but by what happens in Accra, as well.

This is the simple truth of a time when the boundaries between people are overwhelmed by our connections. Your prosperity can expand America's prosperity. Your health and security can contribute to the world's health and security. And the strength of your democracy can help advance human rights for people everywhere.

So I do not see the countries and peoples of Africa as a world apart; I see Africa as a fundamental part of our interconnected world.[23]

President Obama's words reflect the changing world in which Africa finds itself. In this world, African leaders want to rise above the "enterprise of aid," mentioned by President Mkapa, as it currently exists.

Some parts of Africa are still war torn and stuck in the muck of political mismanagement and ethnic conflict as illustrated by the recent conflicts that have engulfed South Sudan, Nigeria, and the Central African Republic. Africa continues to confront the burden of an infrastructure ill suited to the public health problems of the modern world. Africa has yet to get

beyond the infrastructural burden of malaria and AIDS, so it was no surprise that the ebola epidemic was so devastating to several African nations.
There is nothing exceptional about African people that would make them
more susceptible to new diseases. No, the problem in African health is in
large part a problem of a lack of infrastructure to support a robust public
health system. The habit of thinking about health in Africa because of the
epidemic of the day, as in the cases of AIDS and ebola, distorts the reality
of the burden of disease on the continent. It is important to remember that
other communicable diseases, as well as perinatal, maternal, and nutritional
causes, contribute to the majority of all deaths in Africa today. This is not
to say that the epidemic of AIDS and ebola are not important, but only to
suggest that these epidemics would have a different impact if African nations had adequate health care infrastructures.

However, in spite of these setbacks, the bigger story is that of a continent on the rise. It is these signs of hope that are driving the world's attention back toward this neglected and exploited continent. As welcome as
this new awareness is, the solutions to African problems are coming from
Africa. It fact, it may be that Africa will offer solutions to the rest of the
world for problems considered intractable. But first, Africa must lift itself up
from the muck. As Her Excellency Samia Nkrumah said,

> You know, Africa is an immensely rich continent. In fact, our father
> used to say, "poverty in the midst of plenty." Because, we know that
> we have vast resources.
>
> When I say "we," I mean the majority of our people. Maybe a few
> have benefitted over the years, but not the vast majority of the people.
> Hence the fact that after so many years of independence, we have not
> mastered the basic social needs. So the task ahead is to regain control
> of those resources. We will not, we cannot go to war; we will have
> to do that by being very smart. We have to be smart negotiators. But
> what will help us is if we bargain "en masse," in a group. This is simple
> economics, or simple common sense. We know that is where we would
> have some clout, when we are bargaining. And I think we will have to
> do that if we want to maximize on what we have.
>
> At the moment, also, most of our exports are primary products, and
> we know that the equally important, as much as unity is important, we
> also need to, equally importantly, we need to add value to what we are
> exporting. We need to produce more at home. We need to find a way,
> the means and the environment, to enable us to produce more at home.

At a fish market in Dar es Salaam, Tanzania, 2010. Jabari Zuberi/TZ Production Company.

A market in Accra, Ghana, 2011. Jabari Zuberi/TZ Production Company.

With Samia Nkrumah in front of the Kwame Nkrumah Mausoleum and Memorial Park in Accra, Ghana, 2011. Jabari Zuberi/TZ Production Company.

As Kofi Annan noted in his report in 1998, while assistance from the world is crucial to Africa's future, African efforts to change the face of the continent's economy and forms of governance, and Africa's changing relationship with world security, are interconnected with the continent finding its rightful place in the modern world.[24] In both the documentary and this book, we hear from Africans on both sides of this debate and expand the conversation to include other voices and questions about Africa's future, not least how the world can achieve a broader and more realistic engagement with Africa than simply responding to the next famine, disease, disaster, or war.

For me, a person born in the United States, extending African independence requires recognition of how the movement redefines what it means to be human. We started in chapter 1 with Italy arriving in Ethiopia with all of its racist anti-democratic fascism and Africans actively fighting against this rise of fascism. When the fascist focus turned to Europe and Asia, Africa was there to protect and serve. No self-respecting democracy could justify the continued existence of colonialism after World War II. African independence was a fight for African human rights, and as such, it challenged the world to live up to the Universal Declaration of Human Rights that followed World War II. If Africans could lead independent nations, the very idea of second-class citizenship on the basis of race was contradicted. The movement in Africa created a conversation that changed the question and meaning of race in the United States and the world.

French, British, Belgian, Portuguese, Spanish, Italian, and German colonialism were all anti-democratic. It was African independence that brought the possibility of democracy to Africa. Democracy is great; however, alone it will not feed the people, it will not provide health care, and it is often at odds with good old-fashioned capitalism. Good governance requires money, functioning institutions, and a commitment to the common good of the citizens of the nation. Africa is indeed a continent full of wealth. The problem of poverty in Africa is based on its internal underdevelopment and its unequal economic relationships with the world. These problems are accentuated by the lack of African infrastructure.

The Bretton Woods institutions have not served Africa well. The post–World War II economic systems have not fostered African economic development. At the end of World War II, Africans stood with the Allies for the victory against fascism. As a result of World War II, Europe's infrastructure and economies were devastated. As a result, Western Europe got *aid* and *trade* in the form of the Marshall Plan. This was a time when the United States was serious about development and worked to change the world with the creation of the Bretton Woods institutions and NATO. As a result of colonialism, Africa's infrastructure and economies were underdeveloped. Africa got independence, and this independence offered great hope. However, Africa received no Marshall Plan, and when aid did arrive, it came with so many strings that it has become a barrier to development.

The benefits of the African independence movement open a space for reconsidering Africa's place in the world, past and present. This reconsideration needs to happen if a conversation about changing Africa's place in the world will be taken seriously. Africa needs a renaissance to confront twenty-first-century realities. Things can be different for Africa in the twenty-first century, and for this to happen the world and Africa must change. The issue is not if Africa will play a role in the world's future; the conclusion is that Africa is central to America, Europe, Asia, and Latin America's future.

SELECTED CHRONOLOGY
OF EVENTS

This is a chronology of the African art of conducting state affairs. The names of independent African nations, both modern and ancient, are in **boldface**.

BC

2535–2560   Great Pyramid of Khufu constructed at Giza

AD

100–940   Kingdom of **Aksum** (Mangiśta Aksum)
650   The rise of the Arab slave trade in millions of African people

1000s

750–1000   **Ghana Empire** in West Africa
800–1200   First Muslim settlements on east coast of modern Kenya
             Expansion of the African diaspora in Kenya, and the southward direction of Islam from Morocco and Central Maghreb
             Origins of **Yoruba** and **Hausa** states

	Almoravid Empire from northwest Africa and southern Spain
1100	Birth of Timbuktu, the ancient city of trade and education during the days of the **Mali** and **Songhai Empires**
1300	**Mali Empire** prominence
1492–1528	Reign of Askia Mohammed I; **Songhai Empire** prominence
1400	**Wolof Empire** prominence
1443	European slave trade becomes entrenched
1507–1543	Reign of **Bakongo** King Afonso I
1517	Ottoman Turks complete conquest of Egypt

1600s

1637	Dutch take Elmina from the Portuguese and control the Gold Coast
1652	The Dutch establish settlement at **Cape of Good Hope**
1680	**Asante State** prominence

1800s

1800	Great increase in the enslavement of the Zanj from Southeast Africa by the Oman sultanate based in Zanzibar
1804	Independence of **Haiti**, under leadership of Toussant Louverture's former lieutenant, Jean-Jacques Dessalines (successful uprising among the enslaved)
1847	**Liberia** gains independence, July 26
1869	Suez Canal built in Egypt
1880	Samory Taouré reign of the **Wassoulou Empire**
1884–1885	Conference of Berlin almost completely divides Africa among European colonial powers
1885	Invasion of the Congo by Leopold II and the beginning of a period of extreme colonialism
1891	Treaty between Portugal and Britain recognizing the remaining Portuguese colonial territories in Africa
1896	Ethiopians defeat Italians at Battle of Adwa

1897	Ndebele revolt against British in Southern Africa
1898	Rebellion against the colonial hut tax in Sierra Leone
1899–1902	South African ("Boer") War

1900s

1900	Pan-African Conference, London, July
1904	Creation of "French West African Confederation"
	Attempted genocide against Herero and Namaqua begins in German Southwest Africa
1905	Maji-Maji revolt in German East Africa

1910s

1910	**Union of South Africa** established by white minority as they gain independence from Britain, May 31
1912	African National Congress (ANC) formed in South Africa
1914	World War I begins on July 28
1917	Russian Revolution, March 8–November 8
1918	World War I ends on November 11
	Germany loses its African colonies to French and British administration under the authority of the League of Nations
1919	First Pan-African Congress in Paris, February

1920s

1921	Second Pan-African Congress in Paris, London, and Brussels, August and September
1922	Union of Soviet Socialist Republics created on December 30
	Benito Mussolini installed as prime minister of Italy by King Victor Emmanuel III, October 31
	Egypt gains independence, February 23

1923	Third Pan-African Congress in London and Lisbon, November
1927	Fourth Pan-African Congress in New York, August
1929	Aba Women's War in Nigeria

1930s

1933	The Nazi Party becomes the largest elected party in the German Reichstag leading to Adolf Hitler's appointment as Reich chancellor
1935	Fascist Italian troops invade Ethiopia, October 3
1936–1939	Spanish Civil War begins on July 17
1939	Fascist German troops invade Poland, September 1

1940s

1941	End of Italian domination/occupation in **Ethiopia**, May 1
1945	End of World War II, September 2
	Four independent African countries exist after WWII: **Ethiopia**, **Egypt**, **Liberia**, and **South Africa**
	Fifth Pan-African Conference (Manchester, England), October
	The Charter of the United Nations is signed on June 26 in San Francisco at the end of the United Nations Conference on International Organization on October 24
	Setif Uprising, Algeria
1947	India gains independence on August 15
	Beginning of the Cold War
1948	Nationalist party wins election in South Africa and implements apartheid
	Marshall Plan (European Recovery Program) lasts for four years, the program starting in April
	Universal Declaration of Human Rights proclaimed by the United Nations General Assembly in Paris on December 10

1949	People's Republic of China proclaimed, October 1
	Birth of the North Atlantic Treaty Organization (NATO), April 4

1950s

1951	Egypt abrogates treaty with Britain, and British troops occupy Canal Zone
	Libya gains independence on December 24
1952–1959	Mau Mau (Land Freedom Army) uprising in Kenya
	Coup d'état in Egypt
1953	British form Central African Federation (CAF)—Northern Rhodesia, Southern Rhodesia, and Nyasaland—under white minority rule
1954	Coup d'état in Egypt
1955	Release of "Freedom Charter" by ANC and allies
	Bandung Conference in Bandung, Indonesia, April 18–24
	Birth of the Warsaw Pact on May 14. (The Warsaw Pact was a collective defense treaty among eight communist states of Central and Eastern Europe.)
1956	Suez crises in Egypt
	Sudan gains independence on January 1
	Morocco gains independence on March 2
	Tunisia gains independence on March 20
1957	**Ghana** gains independence on March 6 (formerly Gold Coast)
	Coup d'état in Tunisia
1958	**Guinea** gains independence on October 2
	All-African People's Congress in Accra, Ghana, December. (This congress was the first of three conferences following in the spirit of the Fifth Pan-African Congress by calling for the independence of all of Africa. Leaders of the new African republics and freedom fighters attended the congress from the African Independence Movement, along with international supporters.)
	Coup d'état in Sudan

1960s

1960

Year of Africa (seventeen newly independent nations by 1960):

Cameroon, formerly Cameroun (January 1; unified with British Cameroons in 1961)

Togo, formerly French Togoland (April 27)

Mali, formerly French Sudan (June 20)

Senegal (June 20)

Madagascar, formerly French Madagascar (June 26)

Benin, formerly Dahomey (August 1)

Niger, formerly French Niger (August 3)

Burkina Faso, formerly Upper Volta (August 15)

Ivory Coast (August 7)

Chad (August 11)

Central African Republic, formerly Ubangi-Shari (August 13)

Republic of the Congo, formerly Middle Congo (August 15)

Gabon (August 17)

Mauritania (November 28)

Somali, formerly British Somaliland and the Trust Territory of Somalia (July 1)

Nigeria, formerly Federation of Nigeria (October 1)

Democratic Republic of the Congo, formerly Belgian Congo (June 30)

British prime minister Harold Macmillan gives "Wind of Change" speech to parliament of South Africa, February 3

Sharpeville Massacre in South Africa, March 21

Robert Sobukwe arrested and interned after Sharpeville Massacre. (After serving his sentence, he was interned on Robben Island in 1964 with other freedom fighters.)

All-African People's Congress in Tunis, Tunisia, January

1960–1965

Congo crisis (Coups d'état in Congo-Kinshasa in 1960)

1961

W. E. B. Du Bois immigrates to Ghana

Patrice Lumumba murdered in Katanga (Congo), January 17

Sierra Leone gains independence on April 27

Construction of the Berlin Wall started by the German Democratic Republic, August 13

Tanganyika gains independence on December 9 (merged with People's Republic of Zanzibar and Pemba to form the United Republic of Tanzania on April 26, 1964)

All-African People's Congress in Cairo, Egypt, March

1962   **Burundi** gains independence on July 1

Rwanda gains independence on July 1

Algeria gains independence on July 5

Uganda gains independence on October 9

Emperor Haile Selassie incorporates Eritrea into the Ethiopian Empire

Coup d'état in Algeria

1963   Creation of the **Organization of African Unity** (OAU) in Addis Ababa conference of thirty-two independent African states, May 25

Zanzibar gains independence on December 10 (merged with People's Republic of Zanzibar and Pemba to form the United Republic of Tanzania on April 26, 1964)

Kenya gains independence on December 12

Coups d'état in Benin, Congo-Brazzaville, and Togo

1964   OAU summit held in Cairo

Nelson Mandela, Walter Sisulu, and other African freedom fighters get life sentences and are sent to Robben Island

Malawi gains independence on July 6 (formerly Nyasaland)

Zambia gains independence on October 24 (formerly Northern Rhodesia)

Coup d'état in Zanzibar

1965   White minority government makes Unilateral Declaration of Independence in Southern Rhodesia

Gambia gains independence on February 18 (formerly British Gambia)

Coups d'état in Algeria and Congo-Kinshasa, Central African Republic, and Benin

1966   **Botswana** gains independence on September 30 (formerly Bechuanaland Protectorate)

            Lesotho gains independence on October 4 (formerly Basutoland)

            Coups d'état in Nigeria, Ghana, Burkina Faso, Burundi, and Uganda

1967   East African Community formed by Kenya, Tanzania, and Uganda

            The Arusha Declaration on African Socialism and Self-Reliance in Tanzania, February 5

            Egypt defeated by Israel in Six Day War, June 5–10

            Civil war begins in Nigeria (also known as the Biafra War), July 6, 1967–January 15, 1970

            Coups d'état in Sierra Leone, Benin, and Togo

1968   **Equatorial Guinea** gains independence on October 12 (formerly Spanish Guinea)

            Mauritius gains independence on March 12 (formerly British Mauritius)

            Swaziland gains independence on September 6

            Coups d'état in Mali, Congo-Brazzaville, and Sierra Leone

1969   Coups d'état in Somalia, Libya, Sudan, and Benin

                        1970s

1970   Non-Aligned Summit in Lusaka, Zambia

            China begins construction of a 1,100-mile railway linking Tanzania and Zambia—TANZAM (opens in 1976)

1971   Mobutu assumes absolute power in the **Republic of the Congo** and renames the country **Zaire**

            Coup d'état in Uganda

1972   More than one hundred thousand Hutus killed in Burundi

            Idi Amin forces non-citizen Asians to leave Uganda

            Coups d'état in Madagascar, Benin, and Ghana

1973   **Guinea-Bissau** gains independence on September 24

            World hit by fourfold increase in price of oil

            Coup d'état in Rwanda

1974   Coup d'état in Lisbon, Portugal, on April 25; General Spinola recognizes right of African territories to independence

UN General Assembly rejects South Africa's credentials because of its apartheid policies

Twentieth-century coup d'état in Ethiopia (end of rule by Haile Selassie; a second coup in this same year); also a coup d'état in Niger

1975   Independence for Portugal's colonies:

Mozambique on June 25 (formerly Portuguese Mozambique)

Cape Verde on July 5

São Tomé and Príncipe on July 12

Angola on November 11 (formerly Portuguese Angola)

Economic Community of West African States (ECOWAS), founded on May 28

Comoros gains independence on July 6

Coups d'état in Chad, Comoros, Nigeria, and Madagascar

1976   Soweto Uprising in South Africa on June 16

Seychelles gains independence on June 26

Spain relinquishes control of Spanish Sahara. Morocco and Mauritania claim territory.

Coups d'état in Nigeria and Burundi

1977   Ogaden War between Ethiopia and Somalia in July (lasts until March 1978; United States supports Somalia, and the USSR supports Ethiopia)

Djibouti gains independence on June 27

President Bokassa of Central African Republic crowns himself emperor

Coups d'état in Seychelles and Ethiopia

1978   Kenyatta dies, and Arap Moi becomes president of Kenya

Coups d'état in Mauritania, Ghana, and Comoros

1979   Coups d'état in Uganda, Ghana, Equatorial Guinea, Congo-Brazzaville, and Central African Republic

South Africa explodes nuclear weapon in South Atlantic

Coup d'état in Mauritania

1980s

1980	**Zimbabwe** gains independence on April 18 (formerly Rhodesia)
	Southern African Development Coordination Conference (SADCC) formed by frontline states
	Coups d'état in Guinea-Bissau, Liberia, Burkina Faso, Uganda, and Mauritania
1981	HIV epidemic becomes public knowledge
	Other communicable diseases, in addition to perinatal, maternal, and nutritional causes, amount to the majority of all deaths in Africa (especially Africa below the Sahara)
	Coups d'état in Central African Republic and Ghana
1982	US bans import of Libyan oil
	Coups d'état in Burkina Faso and Chad
1983	Coups d'état in Nigeria and Burkina Faso
1984	OAU recognizes the legitimacy of the Sahrawi Arab Democratic Republic (SADR) occupied by Morocco.
	Morocco quits rather than accept OAU decision regarding SADR
	Coups d'état in Guinea and Mauritania
1985	Group of South African business leaders go to Lusaka to meet with Oliver Tambo and other ANC leaders
	Coups d'état in Sudan, Nigeria, and Uganda
1986	Coups d'état in Lesotho and Uganda
1987	Coups d'état in Tunisia, Burkina Faso, and Burundi
1989	Coups d'état in Sudan and Comoros

1990s

1990	End of Cold War
	Nelson Mandela released from prison, February 11
	Namibia gains independence on March 21 (formerly South West Africa)
	Coups d'état in Liberia, Chad, and Lesotho

1990–1992	Fall of the Berlin War and the symbolic end of the Cold War
1991	Collapse of Somalia government
	UN-negotiated cease-fire between Morocco and the Polisario Front in Western Sahara
	Dissolution of the Union of Soviet Socialist Republics (USSR), December 26
	Disbanding of the Warsaw Pact, February 25
	Coups d'état in Mali, Somalia, Ethiopia, and Lesotho
1992	Rio Earth Summit (United Nations Conference on Environment and Development), June 3–14
	US marines deployed in Somalia for "Operation Restore Hope," December 9–May 4
	Coups d'état in Algeria and Sierra Leone
1993	**Eritrea** gains independence, May 24
	Formal establishment of the European Union with the Maastricht Treaty, November 1
	Coup d'état in Nigeria
1994	Genocide in Rwanda, April 7–mid-July
	South Africa gains political independence, April 27. (The African National Congress wins seven of the nine provinces. First act of the newly elected National Assembly is to elect Nelson Mandela as South Africa's first democratically elected president on May 10.)
	The end of classical European colonialism of Africa
	Coups d'état in Gambia and Rwanda
1995	Coups d'état in São Tomé and Príncipe and Comoros
1996	Coups d'état in Burundi, Sierra Leone, and Niger
1997	Coup d'état in Zaire, and Mobutu flees the country on May 16. As the country descends into war, neighboring states (Uganda, Rwanda, Burundi, Angola, Namibia, and Zimbabwe) all take different sides.
	Zimbabwe institutes Land Redistribution Act
	Coups d'état in Congo-Brazzaville and Sierra Leone
1998	Multi-country war in Democratic Republic of the Congo
	US embassy bombings in Kenya and Tanzania, August 7

Coup d'état in Sierra Leone

1999   Coups d'état in Ivory Coast, Niger, Comoros, and Guinea-Bissau

2000S

2001   Four coordinated attacks by al-Qaeda on the United States in New York and Washington, D.C., September 11

President George W. Bush calls for War on Terror in his State of the Union address before the US Congress, September 20

2002   Organization of African Unity renamed the African Union

First prisoners in the US war on terror arrive at Guantanamo Bay detention camp, January 11

2003   Coups d'état in Central African Republic, Guinea-Bissau, and São Tomé and Príncipe

2005   Coup d'état in Mauritania

2008   Coups d'état in Mauritania and Guinea

2009   Coup d'état in Madagascar

2010S

2010   South Africa hosts the World Cup soccer tournament, June 11–July 11

Coup d'état in Niger

2011   **Southern Sudan** gains independence, July 9

Tunisian president Zine El Abidine Ben Ali resigns from power, January

Egyptian president Hosni Mubarak resigns from power, February

Coups d'état in Libya, Egypt, and Tunisia

2012   Coups d'état in Mali and Guinea-Bissau

2013   Coups d'état in Egypt and Central African Republic

2014   Ebola epidemic becomes public knowledge

NOTES

INTRODUCTION

1. Michael Hanchard, "Black Memory versus State Memory: Notes towards a Method," *Small Axe* (Indiana), no. 26 (2008): 45–62.

2. C. Wright Mills, *The Sociological Imagination*, fortieth anniversary edition (originally published in 1959; New York: Oxford University Press, 2000), esp. chap. 8.

3. While I pay some attention to political parties, coalitions, and major events, my focus is on African independence as a social movement. See Mario Diani, "The Concept of Social Movement," *Sociological Review* 40, no. 1 (1992): 1–25.

4. Robin Blackburn, *The Making of New World Slavery: From the Baroque to the Modern, 1492–1800* (London: Verso, 1997), 35, 77–78, 99–112.

5. Georg W. F. Hegel, *The Philosophy of History*, trans. J. Jibree (New York: Dover, 1956).

6. Joseph Chamberlain, "Trade and the Empire," in *Imperial Union and Tariff Reform: Speeches Delivered from May 15th to November 4th by the Right Hon. Joseph Chamberlain, MP* (London: Grant Richards, 1903). Joseph Chamberlain was forced to resign from the cabinet when his colleagues refused to endorse his plan for Imperial Preference Trade in the fall of 1903.

CHAPTER 1: FROM COLONIALISM TO PAN-AFRICANISM

1. John H. Morrow Jr., "Black Africans in World War II: The Soldiers' Stories," *The ANNALS of the American Academy of Political and Social Science Series* 632, no. 1 (2010): 12–25.

2. Mia Fuller, "Wherever You Go, There You Are: Fascist Plans for the Colonial City of Addis Ababa and the Colonizing Suburb of EUR '42," *Journal of*

Contemporary History 31, no. 2 (1996): 397–418; John H. Morrow, *The Great War: An Imperial History* (New York: Routledge, 2004).

3. Haile Selassie, "Appeal to the League of Nations," 1936.

4. George W. Baer, "Sanctions and Security: The League of Nations and the Italian-Ethiopian War, 1935–1936," *International Organization* 27, no. 2 (1973): 165–79; Morrow, "Black Africans in World War II"; Benito Mussolini, "Benito Mussolini's Address on the Invasion of Ethiopia," 1935; Kwame Nkrumah, *Africa Must Unite* (New York: Praeger, 1963); Robin Pickering-Iazzi, "Structures of Feminine Fantasy and Italian Empire Building, 1930–1940," *Italica* 77, no. 3 (2000): 400–17; James C. Robertson, "The Origins of British Opposition to Mussolini over Ethiopia," *Journal of British Studies* 9, no. 1 (1969): 122–42; William R. Scott, "Black Nationalism and the Italo-Ethiopian Conflict, 1934–1936," *The Journal of Negro History* 63, no. 2 (1978): 118–34; Selassie, "Appeal to the League of Nations."

5. Giulia Barrera, "Mussolini's Colonial Race Laws and State–Settler Relations in Africa Orientale Italiana (1935–41)," *Journal of Modern Italian Studies* 8, no. 3 (2003): 425–43; Rainer Baudendistel, "Force versus Law: The International Committee of the Red Cross and Chemical Warfare in the Italo-Ethiopian War 1935–1936," *International Review of the Red Cross*, no. 322 (1998); R. J. B. Bosworth, *Mussolini's Italy: Life Under the Fascist Dictatorship, 1915–1945* (New York: Penguin, 2006), 42; Fuller, "Wherever You Go, There You Are: Fascist Plans for the Colonial City of Addis Ababa and the Colonizing Suburb of EUR '42"; Lina Grip and John Hart, "The Use of Chemical Weapons in the 1935–36 Italo-Ethiopian War," *SIPRI Arms Control and Non-proliferation Programme*, 2009; Richard Pankhurst, "Italian Fascist War Crimes in Ethiopia: A History of Their Discussion, from the League of Nations to the United Nations (1936–1949)," *Northeast African Studies* 6, nos. 1–2 (1999): 83–140; Pickering-Iazzi, "Structures of Feminine Fantasy and Italian Empire Building, 1930–1940"; Selassie, "Appeal to the League of Nations"; Barbara Sòrgoni, "'Defending the Race': The Italian Reinvention of the Hottentot Venus during Fascism," *Journal of Modern Italian Studies* 8, no. 3 (2003): 411–24.

6. The Atlantic Charter, August 14; Foster Rhea Dulles and Gerald E. Ridinger, "The Anti-Colonial Policies of Franklin D. Roosevelt," *Political Science Quarterly* 70, no. 1 (1955): 1–18.

7. Idris S. El-Hareir, "North Africa and the Second World War," in *Africa and the Second World War: Reports and Papers of the Symposium Organized by UNESCO at Benghazi, Libyan Arab Jamahiriya, from 10 to 13 November 1980*, 27–36 (Paris: UNESCO, 1985); Ashley Jackson, "The Imperial Antecedents of British Special Forces," *The RUSI Journal* 154, no. 3 (2009): 62–68.

8. N. Ayele, "The Horn of Africa and Eastern Africa in the World War Decade (1935–45)," in *Africa and the Second World War: Reports and Papers of the Symposium Organized by UNESCO at Benghazi, Libyan Arab Jamahiriya, from 10 to 13 November 1980*, 77–90 (Paris: UNESCO, 1985); David Killingray, "Military and Labour Recruitment in the Gold Coast during the Second World War," *The Journal of African*

History 23, no. 1 (1982): 83–95; Vincent Bakpetu Thompson, *Africa and Unity: The Evolution of Pan-Africanism* (London: Longman, 1969).

9. Myron J. Echenberg, *Colonial Conscripts: The Tirailleurs Sénégalais in French West Africa, 1857–1960* (Portsmouth, NH: Heinemann, 1991); Jan H. Hofmeyr, "Germany's Colonial Claims: A South African View," *Foreign Affairs* 17, no. 4 (1939): 788–98; Thomas C. Martin, "The Vichy Government and French Colonial Prisoners of War, 1940–1944," *French Historical Studies* 25, no. 4 (2002): 657–92; Morrow, "Black Africans in World War II."

10. For a transcription of these transformations, see chapter 1 of Tony Judt, *Postwar: A History of Europe since 1945* (New York: Penguin, 2005).

11. Examples of this can be found in the experience of the Germans in Namibia (Horst Drechsler, "The Herero Uprising," in *The History and Sociology of Genocide: Analyses and Case Studies*, ed. Frank Chalk and Kurt Jonassohns, 231–48 [New Haven, CT: Yale University Press]), the British in Kenya (Caroline Elkins, *Imperial Reckoning* [New York: Henry Holt, 2005]), and the Belgians in the Congo (Adam Hochschild, *King Leopold's Ghost* [New York: Marier Books, 1998]).

12. Judt, *Postwar*, chap. 1.

13. Thompson, *Africa and Unity*, 107.

14. Echenberg, *Colonial Conscripts*; Judt, *Postwar*, 283; Manfred Halpern, "The Algerian Uprising of 1945," *Middle East Journal* 2, no. 2 (1948): 191–202.

15. W. E. B. Du Bois, *The World and Africa: An Inquiry into the Part Which Africa has Played in World History* (New York: Viking, 1947), 242; David Levering Lewis, *W. E. B. Du Bois: The Fight for Equality and the American Century, 1919–1963* (New York: Henry Holt, 2000); Morrow, "Black Africans in World War II"; Thompson, *Africa and Unity*.

16. Levering Lewis, *W. E. B. Du Bois*, 501; Herbert Aptheker, *The Correspondence of W. E. B. Du Bois*, vol. 2, *Selections, 1934–1944* (Amherst: University of Massachusetts Press, 1997); Aptheker, *The Correspondence of W. E. B. Du Bois*, vol. 3, *Selections, 1944–1963* (Amherst: University of Massachusetts Press).

17. Du Bois, *The World and Africa*; Levering Lewis, *W. E. B. Du Bois: The Fight for Equality*. Paris was also considered as a congressional location, and then London was selected because of its political activism and labor movement. Finally, attendees met in Manchester, England, as London was in a state of rebuilding post–World War II.

18. Also known as the Washington Conversations on International Peace and Security Organization.

19. Carol Anderson, "From Hope to Disillusion: African Americans, the United Nations, and the Struggle for Human Rights, 1944–1947," *Diplomatic History* 20, no. 4 (1996): 531–63; W. E. B. Du Bois, *Color and Democracy: Colonies and Peace* (New York: Harcourt, Brace, 1945).

20. Peter Abrahams, *The Black Experience in the 20th Century: An Autobiography and Meditation* (Bloomington: Indiana University Press, 2001); Levering Lewis, *W. E. B. Du Bois: The Fight for Equality*, 513.

CHAPTER 2: THE END OF COLONIAL RULE

1. Ieuan Griffiths, "The Scramble for Africa: Inherited Political Boundaries," *Geographical Journal* 152, no. 2 (1986): 204–16; St. Clair Drake, "Diaspora Studies and Pan-Africanism," in *Global Dimensions of the African Diaspora*, ed. Joseph E. Harris, 2nd ed., 451–514 (Washington, DC: Howard University Press, 1993); G. Wesley Johnson, "The Ascendancy of Blaise Diagne and the Beginning of African Politics in Senegal," *Africa* 35, no. 3 (1996): 235–53; J. Ayo Langley, "Pan-Africanism in Paris, 1924–36," *Journal of Modern African Studies* 7, no. 1 (1969): 69–94; Paul Nugent, *Africa since Independence: A Comparative History*, 2nd ed. (New York: Palgrave Macmillan, 2012), 14–15; David Killingray, "Military and Labour Recruitment in the Gold Coast during the Second World War," *The Journal of African History* 23, no. 1 (1982), 83–95.

2. W. E. B. Du Bois, *The World and Africa: An Inquiry into the Part Which Africa has Played in World History* (New York: Viking, 1947), chap. 1.

3. David Birmingham, *The Decolonization of Africa* (London: UCL Press, 1995), 4–5.

4. Nugent, *Africa since Independence*, 18–19.

5. Birmingham, *The Decolonization of Africa*, 3–4; Nugent, *Africa since Independence*, 26–27.

6. Immanuel Wallerstein, *Africa: The Politics of Independence and Unity* (Lincoln: University of Nebraska Press, 2005).

7. Du Bois, *Africa and the World*, 1.

8. P. J. Cain and A. G. Hopkins, *British Imperialism: Crisis and Deconstruction, 1914–1990* (New York: Longman, 1993); also Nugent, *Africa since Independence*, 26–27.

9. Robert L. Tignor, *Capitalism and Nationalism at the End of Empire* (Princeton, NJ: Princeton University Press, 1997).

10. C.-R. Ageron, "Developments in North Africa during the Second World War," in *Africa and the Second World War: Reports and Papers of the Symposium Organized by UNESCO at Benghazi, Libyan Arab Jamahiriya, from 10 to 13 November 1980*, 37–50 (Paris: UNESCO, 1985); Adrienne M. Israel, "Ex-Servicemen at the Crossroads: Protest and Politics in Post-War Ghana," *Journal of Modern African Studies* 30, no. 2 (1992): 359–68; J. J. Milewski, "The Second World War in Volume III of the General History of Africa," in *Africa and the Second World War: Reports and Papers of the Symposium Organized by UNESCO at Benghazi, Libyan Arab Jamahiriya, from 10 to 13 November 1980*, 123–32 (Paris: UNESCO, 1985); Sylvanus E. Olympio, "Togo: Problems and Progress of a New Nation," *Africa Today* 7, no. 2 (1960): 5–7; Robert I. Rotberg, "The Rise of African Nationalism: The Case of East and Central Africa," *World Politics* 15, no. 1 (1962): 75–90; Richard L. Sklar, *Nigerian Political Parties: Power in an Emergent African Nation* (Trenton, NJ: Africa World Press, 2004); Vincent Bakpetu Thompson, *Africa and Unity: The Evolution of Pan-Africanism* (London: Longman, 1969), 84, 91–92.

11. Thompson, *Africa and Unity*.

12. Nugent, *Africa since Independence*, 22; Thompson, *Africa and Unity*, 66–67.

13. Birmingham, *The Decolonization of Africa*, 13; Thompson, *Africa and Unity*, 71–77; Eve Troutt Powell, *A Different Shade of Colonialism: Egypt, Great Britain, and the Mastery of the Sudan* (Berkeley: University of California Press, 2003).

14. Birmingham, *The Decolonization of Africa*, 14–15.

15. Myron Echenberg, *Colonial Conscripts: The Tirailleurs Sénégalais in French West Africa, 1857–1960* (Portsmouth, NH: Heinemann, 1991); Adrienne M. Israel, "Ex-Servicemen at the Crossroads: Protest and Politics in Post-War Ghana," *Journal of Modern African Studies* 30, no. 2 (1992): 359–68.

16. Ageron, "Developments in North Africa during the Second World War," 40; L. Carl Brown, "Bourguiba and Bourguibism Revisited: Reflections and Interpretation," *Middle East Journal* 55, no. 1 (2001): 43–57; Martin Evans, "Guy Mollet's Third Way: National Renewal and the French Civilising Mission," *French History and Civilisation* 2 (2009): 169–80; Clement Henry Moore, "The Neo-Destour Party of Tunisia: A Structure for Democracy?," *World Politics* 14, no. 3 (1962): 461–82; Powell, *A Different Shade of Colonialism*.

17. Ageron, "Developments in North Africa during the Second World War"; Keith Callard, "The Republic of Bourguiba," *International Journal* 16, no. 1 (1960/1961): 17–36; E. G. H. Joffe, "The Moroccan Nationalist Movement: Istiqlal, the Sultan, and the Country," *Journal of African History* 26, no. 4 (1985): 289–307; Tony Judt, *Postwar: A History of Europe since 1945* (New York: Penguin, 2005), 286; Thomas Riegler, "The State as a Terrorist: France and the Red Hand," *Perspectives on Terrorism* 6, no. 6 (2012): 22–33; L. B. Ware, "Habib Bourguiba," in *Political Leaders of the Contemporary Middle East and North Africa: A Biographical Dictionary*, ed. Bernard Reich, 119–26 (Westport, CT: Greenwood); Powell, *A Different Shade of Colonialism*.

18. Birmingham, *The Decolonization of Africa*, 5.

19. Birmingham, *The Decolonization of Africa*, 27–29; Nugent, *Africa since Independence*, 27–29.

20. Thompson, *Africa and Unity*, 91–92.

21. Thompson, *Africa and Unity*, 92–94.

22. Robert Addo-Fening, "Gandhi and Nkrumah: A Study of Non-violence and Non-cooperation Campaigns in India and Ghana as an Anti-colonial Strategy," *Transactions of the Historical Society of Ghana* 13, no. 1 (1972): 65–85.

23. Kwame Nkrumah, *Ghana: The Autobiography of Kwame Nkrumah* (New York: International Publishers, 1979); Nugent, *Africa since Independence*, 27–28; Thompson, *Africa and Unity*, 92.

24. Addo-Fening, "Gandhi and Nkrumah," 83; Nkrumah, *Ghana*, 135; Thompson, *Africa and Unity*, 94.

25. Nkrumah, *Ghana*, 138.

26. Ibid.; Rupe Simms, "'I Am a Non-Denominational Christian and a Marxist Socialist': A Gramscian Analysis of the Convention People's Party and Kwame Nkrumah's Use of Religion," *Sociology of Religion* 64, no. 4 (2003): 463–77.

27. Akwasi B. Assensoh, *African Political Leadership: Jomo Kenyatta, Kwame Nkrumah, and Julius K. Nyerere* (Malabar, FL: Krieger, 1998).

28. Nugent, *Africa since Independence*, 28; S. A. de Smith, "The Independence of Ghana," *Modern Law Review* 20, no. 4 (1957): 347–63.

29. Kevin K. Gaines, *American Africans in Ghana: Black Expatriates and the Civil Rights Era* (Chapel Hill: University of North Carolina Press), 2.

30. Judt, *Postwar*; Vijay Prashad, *The Darker Nations: A People's History of the Third World* (New York: New Press, 2007).

31. Gaines, *American Africans in Ghana*, 2; Thompson, *Africa and Unity*, 64.

32. Prashad, *The Darker Nations*; Thompson, *Africa and Unity*.

33. Aimé Césaire, in *Political Thought of Sékou Touré*, Présence Africaine, no. 29 (December 1959–January 1960), 63. Also see June Milne, *Sekou Toure* (London: Panaf Books, 1978).

34. Thompson, *Africa and Unity*, 86–87.

35. Ibid., chap. 9.

36. Babacar M'Baye, "Richard Wright and African Francophone Intellectuals: A Reassessment of the 1956 Congress of Black Writers in Paris," *African and Black Diaspora: An International Journal* 2, no. 1 (2009): 29–42; Charles S. Rhyne, "Law in Africa: A Report on the Lagos Conference," *American Bar Association Journal* 47, no. 7 (1961): 685–88.

37. Frank Myers, "Harold Macmillan's 'Winds of Change' Speech: A Case Study in the Rhetoric of Policy Change," *Rhetoric & Public Affairs* 3, no. 4 (2000): 555–75.

38. Ibid., 565.

39. David Anderson, *Histories of the Hanged: The Dirty War in Kenya and the End of Empire* (New York: Norton), 27–28.

40. Prashad, *The Darker Nations*, 4, 33–36.

41. Evans, "Guy Mollet's Third Way," 170, 174; Judt, *Postwar*, 286; Prashad, *The Darker Nations*, 4–5.

42. Ted Morgan, *My Battle of Algiers* (New York: HarperCollins, 2005).

43. Irwin Wall, "De Gaulle, the 'Anglo-Saxons,' and the Algerian War," *Journal of Strategic Studies* 25, no. 2 (2002): 118–37.

44. Judt, *Postwar*, 286–88.

45. Prashad, *The Darker Nations*, 121–22; Neelan Srivastava, "Anti-colonial Violence and the 'Dictatorship of Truth' in the Films of Gillo Pontecorvo," *Interventions: International Journal of Postcolonial Studies* 7, no. 1 (2005): 97–106.

46. Anderson, *Histories of the Hanged*, 3, 63, 230–34.

47. For more about the Land and Freedom Army, see Kenneth Good, "Settler Colonialism: Economic Development and Class Formation," *Journal of Modern African Studies* 14, no. 4 (1976): 597–620.

48. See Anderson, *Histories of the Hanged*, esp. chaps. 1 and 2.

49. Ibid., 4–5, 10, 288.

50. Anderson, *Histories of the Hanged*, 290, 314, 329; Annie E. Coombes, "Monumental Histories: Commemorating Mau Mau with the Statue of Dedan Kimathi," *African Studies* 70, no. 2 (2011): 202–23.

51. Judt, *Postwar*, 513; Norman Macqueen, "Portugal and Africa: The Politics of Re-Engagement," *Journal of Modern African Studies* 23, no. 1 (1985): 31–51; Godfrey Mwakikagile, *Africa after Independence: Realities of Nationhood*, 3rd ed. (Dar es Salaam: New Africa Press, 2009).

52. For more about Cabral and his ideas, see Amílcar Cabral, *National Liberation and Culture* (Syracuse, NY: Syracuse University, 1970); Prashad, *The Darker Nations*, 111–15.

CHAPTER 3: AFRICA IN THE COLD WAR

1. John Lewis Gaddis, *The Cold War: A New History* (New York: Penguin, 2006).

2. Giovanni Arrighi, "The Global Market," *Journal of World-Systems Research* 5, no. 2 (Summer 1999): 217–51.

3. For a similar argument, see Odd Arne Westad's *The Global Cold War: Third World Interventions and the Making of Our Times* (New York: Cambridge University Press, 2007), especially chaps. 1 and 2 in which he describes the United States as an empire of freedom and liberty, and the Soviet Union as an empire of justice, hence human rights. Also see Samuel Moyn's book, *The Last Utopia: Human Rights in History* (New York: Belknap Press, 2012).

4. Tony Judt, *Postwar: A History of Europe since 1945* (New York: Penguin, 2005); Theodore Meron, "On a Hierarchy of International Human Rights," *American Journal of International Law* 80, no. 1 (1986): 1–23; W. E. B. Du Bois, *The World and Africa: Inquiry into the Part Which Africa Has Played in World History* (New York: Viking, 1947), chap. 1.

5. David Birmingham, *The Decolonization of Africa* (London: UCL Press, 1995); Judt, *Postwar*; Vijay Prashad, *The Darker Nations: A People's History of the Third World* (New York: New Press, 2007); Vincent Bakpetu Thompson, *Africa and Unity: The Evolution of Pan-Africanism* (London: Longman, 1969).

6. Harold Macmillan, "Harold Macmillan: 'Winds of Change,' 1960," in *The Cold War: A History in Documents and Eyewitness Accounts*, ed. Jussi M. Hanhimäki and Odd Arne Westad, 356–58 (Oxford: Oxford University Press, 2004), 357.

7. Judt, *Postwar*.

8. John F. Kennedy, "Kennedy on the Significance of Berlin, June 1963," in *The Cold War: A History in Documents and Eyewitness Accounts*, edited by Jussi M. Hanhimäki and Odd Arne Westad, 330–31 (Oxford: Oxford University Press, 2004), 330.

9. Mark Twain, *King Leopold's Soliloquy* (New York: International Publishing, 1971).

10. Adam Hochschild, *King Leopold's Ghost: A Story of Greed, Terror, and Heroism in Colonial Africa* (New York: Houghton Mifflin Harcourt, 1999); Twain, *King Leopold's Soliloquy.*

11. Ludo De Witte, *The Assassination of Lumumba* (New York: Verso, 2002), 1–3; Hochschild, *King Leopold's Ghost*; David Renton, David Seddon, and Leo Zeilig, *The Congo: Plunder & Resistance* (New York: Zed Books, 2007), 81; Thompson, *Africa and Unity.*

12. De Witte, *The Assassination of Lumumba*; Hochschild, *King Leopold's Ghost*; William H. Worger, Nancy L. Clark, and Edward A. Alpers, eds., *Africa and the West: A Documentary History*, vol. 2, *From Colonialism to Independence, 1875 to the Present*, 2nd ed. (New York: Oxford University Press, 2010), 136.

13. De Witte, *The Assassination of Lumumba*; Worger, Clark, and Alpers, *Africa and the West*, 138.

14. De Witte, *The Assassination of Lumumba*; Richard Iton, *In Search of the Black Fantastic: Politics and Popular Culture in the Post–Civil Rights Era* (New York: Oxford University Press, 2008); Kevin A. Spooner, *Canada, the Congo Crisis, and UN Peacekeeping, 1960–64* (Vancouver: University of British Columbia Press, 2009).

15. Adlai E. Stevenson, *Looking Outward: Years of Crisis at the United Nations*, ed. Robert L. Schiffer and Selma Schiffer (New York: Harper and Row, 1963), 13–14.

16. Hochschild, *King Leopold's Ghost*; David F. Schmitz, *The United States and Right Wing Dictatorships, 1965–1989* (New York: Cambridge University Press, 2006).

17. Richard M. Nixon, "Remarks of Welcome to President Joseph Desire Mobutu of the Democratic Republic of the Congo: August 4, 1970," in *Public Papers of the Presidents of the United States: Richard Nixon*, 644–45 (Washington, DC: GPO, 1971), 644–45.

18. Ibid, 645.

19. Colin Legum, "The Organisation of African Unity—Success or Failure?," *International Affairs* 51, no. 2 (1975): 208–19; Nathan M. Shamuyarira, "The Lusaka Manifesto on Southern Africa, Lusaka 14th–16th April 1969: Full Text Commentary on the Lusaka Manifesto," *African Review* 1, no. 1 (1971): 66–79.

20. See Odd Arne Westad's *The Global Cold War: Third World Interventions and the Making of Our Times.*

21. Stephen Ellis, "The Genesis of the ANC's Armed Struggle in South Africa 1948–1961," *Journal of Southern African Studies*, 37, no. 4 (2011): 657–76; William Mervin Gumede, *Thabo Mbeki and the Battle for the Soul of the ANC* (London: Zed Books, 2007); Christabel Gurney, "'A Great Cause': The Origins of the Anti-Apartheid Movement, June 1959–March 1960," *Journal of Southern African Studies* 26, no. 1 (2000): 123–44.

22. Gumede, *Thabo Mbeki*; Sedick Isaacs, *Surviving in the Apartheid Prison: Robben Island; Flash Backs of an Earlier Life* (Bloomington, IN: Xlibris, 2010); Charmaine

McEachern, "Mapping the Memories: Politics, Place and Identity in the District Six Museum, Cape Town," *Social Identities: Journal for the Study of Race, Nation and Culture* 4, no. 3 (1998): 499–521.

23. Nelson Mandela, *Long Walk to Freedom: The Autobiography of Nelson Mandela* (Boston: Little, Brown, 1994); Anthony Sampson, *Mandela: The Authorised Biography* (London: HarperCollins, 2000), 148; Alan Wieder, *Ruth First and Joe Slovo in the War against Apartheid* (New York: Monthly Review Press, 2013).

24. Gumede, *Thabo Mbeki*; Mandela, *Long Walk to Freedom*; Manning Marable and Peniel Joseph, "Steve Biko and the International Context of Black Consciousness," in *Biko Lives! Contesting the Legacies of Steve Biko*, ed. Andile Mngxitama, Amanda Alexander, and Nigel C. Gibson, vii–x (New York: Palgrave Macmillan, 2008); Andile Mngxitama, Amanda Alexander, and Nigel C. Gibson, "Biko Lives," in *Biko Lives! Contesting the Legacies of Steve Biko*, ed. Andile Mngxitama, Amanda Alexander, and Nigel C. Gibson, 1–20 (New York: Palgrave Macmillan, 2008); Aelred Stubbs, "Introduction," in *Steve Biko 1946–77: I Write What I Like*, ed. Aelred Stubbs, 1–2 (Johannesburg, South Africa, 1987).

25. Mandela, *Long Walk to Freedom*.

26. Steve Biko on German television. Also see Steve Biko, "Our Strategy for Liberation," in *Steve Biko 1946–77: I Write What I Like*, ed. Aelred Stubbs, 143–51 (Johannesburg, South Africa, 1987), 144–48; Mngxitama, Alexander, and Gibson, "Biko Lives"; Stubbs, "Introduction."

27. Ronald Reagan, "Address to the 39th Session of the United Nations General Assembly in New York, New York: September 24, 1984," in *Public Papers of the Presidents of the United States: Ronald Reagan, Book II—June 30 to December 31, 1984*, 1355–61 (Washington, DC: GPO, 1987), 1357.

28. Ronald Reagan, "Remarks on East-West Relations at the Brandenburg Gate in West Berlin: June 12, 1987," in *Public Papers of the Presidents of the United States: Ronald Reagan, Book I—January 1 to July 3, 1987*, 634–38 (Washington, DC: GPO, 1989), 635.

CHAPTER 4: APRIL 1994 AND BEYOND

1. David Anderson, *Histories of the Hanged: The Dirty War in Kenya and the End of Empire* (New York: Norton, 2005); David Birmingham, *The Decolonization of Africa* (London: UCL Press, 1995); Tony Judt, *Postwar: A History of Europe since 1945* (New York: Penguin, 2005); Nelson Mandela, *Long Walk to Freedom: The Autobiography of Nelson Mandela* (Boston: Little, Brown, 1994); Immanuel Wallerstein, *Africa: The Politics of Independence and Unity* (Lincoln: University of Nebraska Press, 2005).

2. Nelson Mandela, *The Struggle Is My Life* (Bombay: Popular Prakashan, 1990), 217; Mandela, *Long Walk to Freedom*.

3. Mandela, *Long Walk to Freedom*.

4. Mandela, *Long Walk to Freedom*; Philip Verwimp, "Death and Survival during the 1994 Genocide in Rwanda," *Population Studies* 58, no. 2 (2004): 233–45.

5. Alex Boraine, *A Country Unmasked: Inside South Africa's Truth and Reconciliation Commission* (Oxford: Oxford University Press, 2000); Richard A. Wilson, *The Politics of Truth and Reconciliation in South Africa: Legitimizing the Post-Apartheid State* (Cambridge: Cambridge University Press, 2001).

6. Nelson Mandela, "Remarks by President Clinton and President Nelson Mandela at African American Religious Leaders Reception," White House Office of the Press Secretary, September 22, 1998, official video courtesy William J. Clinton Library.

7. Roy Joseph, "The New World Order: President Bush and the Post–Cold War Era," in *The Rhetorical Presidency of George H. W. Bush*, ed. Martin J. Medhurst, 81–101 (College Station: Texas A & M University Press, 2006); Judt, *Postwar*; Paul Nugent, *Africa since Independence: A Comparative History*, 2nd ed. (New York: Palgrave Macmillan, 2012).

8. Birmingham, *The Decolonization of Africa*; David Theo Goldberg, *The Racial State* (Malden, MA: Blackwell, 2002); Charles W. Mills, *The Racial Contract* (Ithaca, NY: Cornell University Press, 1997); Andile Mngxitama, Amanda Alexander, and Nigel C. Gibson, "Biko Lives," in *Biko Lives! Contesting the Legacies of Steve Biko*, ed. Andile Mngxitama, Amanda Alexander, and Nigel C. Gibson, 1–20 (New York: Palgrave Macmillan, 2008); Kwame Nkrumah, *Ghana: The Autobiography of Kwame Nkrumah* (New York: International Publishers, 1979); Tukufu Zuberi, *Thicker than Blood: How Racial Statistics Lie* (Minneapolis: University of Minnesota Press, 2001).

9. Mills, *The Racial Contract*; Nugent, *Africa since Independence*; Wallerstein, *Africa*.

10. Mahmood Mamdani, *When Victims Become Killers: Colonialism, Nativism, and the Genocide in Rwanda* (Princeton, NJ: Princeton University Press, 2001).

11. Anderson, *Histories of the Hanged*; Nugent, *Africa*; William H. Worger, Nancy L. Clark, and Edward A. Alpers, eds., *Africa and the West: A Documentary History*, vol. 2, *From Colonialism to Independence, 1875 to the Present*, 2nd ed. (New York: Oxford University Press, 2010).

12. Nic Cheesman, "The Kenyan Elections of 2007: An Introduction," *Journal of Eastern African Studies* 2, no. 2 (2008): 166–84; Gabrielle Lynch and Misa Zgonec-Rozej, *The ICC Intervention in Kenya* (London: Chatham House, 2013).

13. Nugent, *Africa*; and Gérard Prunier, *Africa's World War: Congo, the Rwandan Genocide, and the Making of a Continental Catastrophe* (New York: Oxford University Press, 2009).

14. See Rogaia Mustafa Abusharaf, "Debating Darfur in the World," *The ANNALS of the American Academy of Political and Social Science Series* 632, no. 1 (2010): 63–85.

15. Princeton N. Lyman and J. Stephen Morrison, "The Terrorist Threat in Africa," *Foreign Affairs* 83, no. 1 (2004): 75–86; Ruth Wedgwood, "Responding

to Terrorism: The Strikes against Bin Laden," *Yale Journal of International Law* 24 (1999): 559–76.

16. Barack Obama, "Remarks by the President at the United States Military Academy Commencement Ceremony" (The White House, Office of the Press Secretary, 2014).

17. See Charles R. Stith, "Radical Islam in East Africa," *The ANNALS of the American Academy of Political and Social Science* 632, no. 1 (2010): 55–66, for a discussion of the likely implications of this type of policy on the war against terrorism.

18. See Rogaia Mustafa Abusharaf, "Debating Darfur in the World," *The ANNALS of the American Academy of Political and Social Science Series* 632, no. 1 (2010): 63–85.

19. See Graham Hancock, *Lords of Poverty: The Power, Prestige, and Corruption of the International Aid Business* (New York: Atlantic Monthly Press, 1989); William Easterly, *The White Man's Burden: Why the West's Efforts to Aid the Rest Have Done So Much Ill and So Little Good* (New York: Penguin, 2006); Dambisa Moya, *Dead Aid: Why Aid Is Not Working and How There Is a Better Way for Africa* (New York: Farrar, Straus and Giroux, 2010) for the anti–Western aid argument, and Jeffrey D. Sachs, *The End of Poverty: Economic Possibilities for Our Time* (New York: Penguin, 2005), and Paul Collier, *The Bottom Billion: Why the Poorest Countries Are Failing and What Can Be Done about It* (Oxford: Oxford University Press, 2007) for the pro–Western aid advocates.

20. Birmingham, *The Decolonization of Africa*; Nkrumah, *Ghana.*

21. Kwame Nkrumah, *Africa Must Unite* (New York: Frederick A. Praeger, 1963), xi.

22. Yun Sun, "Africa in China's Foreign Policy," Brookings, April 2014.

23. Barack Obama, "Remarks by the President to the Ghanaian Parliament" (The White House, Office of the Press Secretary, 2009).

24. Kofi Annan, *The Causes of Conflict and the Promotion of Durable Peace and Sustainable Development in Africa*, Report of the Secretary General (New York: United Nations, A/52/871, S/1998/318, April 1998).

INDEX